Physical Expression and the Performing Artist

Physical Expression

and the

Performing Artist

Moving Beyond the Plateau

Jerald Schwiebert
with Candace Platt

The University of Michigan Press • Ann Arbor

Published in the United States of America by
The University of Michigan Press
Manufactured in the United States of America
♾ Printed on acid-free paper

2015   2014   2013   2012   4   3   2   1

A CIP catalog record for this book is available from the British Library.

Library of Congress Cataloging-in-Publication Data

Schwiebert, Jerald.
    Physical expression and the performing artist : moving beyond the
plateau / Jerald Schwiebert with Candace Platt.
        p.   cm.
    Includes bibliographical references and index.
    ISBN 978-0-472-03416-1 (pbk. : alk. paper)
    1. Movement (Acting) 2. Mind and body. I. Platt, Candace. II.
Title.
PN2071.M6.S39 2011
792.02'8 — dc22   2011003376

Contents

Preface

You can observe a lot just by watching.
—YOGI BERRA

In the 1970s, when I was living in New York, I made a daily commute by subway from Forest Hills in Queens to midtown, where I worked as an assistant film editor. The forms and shapes of the commuters traveling to and from Manhattan fascinated me—particularly their physicality and the patterns of tension that I saw in their bodies—and I began to make sketches of them. At that time, I had no idea that such observations would become a major focus of my life.

Years later, when I entered the graduate directing program at the Theatre Department of the University of California, San Diego, La Jolla, I became fascinated with the voice, movement, and acting classes that at that time were part of the graduate directing curriculum. Following graduation, I taught acting and directing at various colleges, universities, and conservatories. In my teaching, I began to notice how student actors, try as they might to advance to the next level of artistry, would sooner or later reach a plateau beyond which they could not progress. This was a puzzle I decided I would try to solve.

By observing these students and their bodies much as I had the subway commuters in New York, I began to see that the things holding them back were physical habits and familiar postures, combined with the tension of performing. The obstacles were things that student performers hadn't considered or had an awareness of but that precluded their progress: they were in their own way and didn't know it.

My graduate training exposed me to a variety of movement disciplines, including Laban, Alexander, and Feldenkrais, as well as to the fundamentals of ballet and Afro-Cuban dance. Since that time, I have taken classes in yoga, modern and jazz dance, and drawing, all of which contributed to my knowledge of the body. Later I studied the principles of tai chi, the Alexander Technique, Rolfing (Structural Integration), Pilates, Trager, sports speed training, plyometrics, kinesiology, and basic anatomy and physiology.

You don't have to be a genius to figure out that at their most basic level, these disciplines are talking about the same thing and address the same problems. I could quickly see that by selecting elements from each of these disciplines and synthesizing them into one, I could devise an approach specifically designed to deal with the problem of tension while performing.

These principles are so universal that they will work for any performing artist or for anyone who wants to improve the efficiency of physical activity, whether it is performing, conducting, giving a presentation, or simply getting out of a chair.

It seems to me that great performers are first and foremost good movers.

For the past twenty years I have taught at the School of Music, Theatre and Dance at the University of Michigan. More recently my career has expanded into one as a performance coach, helping performing artists of all types, including flute players, string players, voice majors and opera singers, symphony and wind conductors, and instrumentalists of all kinds.

Through these experiences and years of teaching, I began to see that the two great evils of performing, the fear of failure and the desire to do a good job, affected everyone, not just actors, and that the problems were universal to all the performing arts—and perhaps to all of life.

Fortunately, my training in theater gave me a way of thinking about this problem, derived from the Stanislavski acting method that I had studied in graduate school. The famous Russian acting teacher created a method, a way for us to be authentic while performing. The secret underlying his method is to do what is doable. This method gave me the last puzzle pieces, by adding the useful element of performance theory to my approach.

To move forward we need not only a dynamic body but also an approach to performing that allows the performer's body to be dynamic.

Physical Expression and the Performing Artist is an introduction, a primer for expanding your capacity for physical expression. It was developed from my study, from the classes and workshops that I have taught. These fundamentals will work for anyone, from any discipline. This book attempts to develop or synthesize a language of physical expression based on my experience and observations over several decades. I am convinced that if you were to engage in a similar study, the ideas are so obvious that you, too, would come to the same conclusions.

This book is designed to help you find in yourself the body that is more able to respond, to help you get the tension out of your body so that you might transcend to the next level of your artistry.

I wish to thank all those who have gone before, who have developed these ideas, and my teachers whose work, study, and generosity have so greatly influenced my life and made this book possible.

Jerald Schwiebert

Acknowledgments

Many people have helped and contributed in different ways to the development this book. To all of you, thank you.

I want to especially thank Candace Platt for her contributions and assistance during the writing and editing processes, for her determination, and for her friendship.

Thanks also to Richard Avsharian for the summer he spent researching and helping out with whatever was needed on the manuscript, and to Mark Leventner, Melissa Gross, Dot Coyne, and Bernie Coyne for their valuable feedback on the manuscript as it was taking shape.

I'd also like to thank my teachers and my students. Thanks especially to those who took time out of your lives to serve as models for the drawings.

This book, like my teaching, draws from a wide variety of techniques and approaches, so many that it is impossible to mention all of them. In the area of performance theory, I am indebted to the work of Constantin Stanislavski, Richard Boleslavski, Viola Spolin, and my mentors, Arthur Wagner and Alan Schneider. In the study of human anatomy, the work of George B. Bridgeman, I. A. Kapandji, and Blandine Calais-Germain has particularly informed my own. In the study of movement techniques and practices, I have benefited from the teachings in Tai Chi of Harold Lee; the body work of Ida Rolf, Rudolf Laban, Moshe Feldekrais, and F. M. Alexander (and in particular my teachers of The Alexander Technique Foundation, Philadelphia); and finally, I owe a debt to the generosity of Bill Conable and Barbara Conable for introducing and sharing with me their concept of body mapping.

Thanks also to the University of Michigan School of Music, Theatre and Dance, Department of Theatre, for their encouragement and support, and to everyone at the University of Michigan Press, particularly LeAnn Fields and Christina Milton.

Illustrations

Dorothea Lange's photo "Wife of a Migratory Laborer with Three Children," June 1938, from the Library of Congress, Prints and Photographs Division. Michelangelo, *Studies for the Libyan Sibyl* on pages 6, 13, and 31 from The

Metropolitan Museum of Art. Purchase, Joseph Pulitzer Bequest, 1924 (24.197.2). Image © The Metropolitan Museum of Art. Advertising photo of mother and daughter on the telephone on pages 5, 11, and 133 courtesy Kaye Bennett of the Upjohn Company. Anatomical drawings by Bernhard Albinus (1697–1770) throughout the book are from the National Library of Medicine, Washington, D.C.

Introduction

We must reconsider what is meant by "talent." It is highly possible that what is called talented behavior is simply a greater individual capacity for experiencing. From this point of view, it is in the increasing of the individual capacity for experiencing that the untold potentiality of a personality can be evoked.

—VIOLA SPOLIN, *Improvisation for the Theater*

Long Book/Short Book

When you teach or learn movement (or anything for that matter), there are two approaches you can use. I call them the "Short Book" and the "Long Book." The Short Book is the how-to book, and the Long Book is the how-*not*-to book.

The Long Book works with symptoms rather than causes. Quite often the pedagogy of the Long Book addresses a particular symptom that was giving a performer trouble at a given point in his or her training.

For example, perhaps a student is looking at the ground while he or she performs. So he or she is told to look above the last row. This fixes the problem of looking at the ground. But now the head is fixed, literally stuck in this "correct" position. Now

the neck and other body parts become the problem.

Unfortunately, when you deal with symptoms and not the cause, the adjustment often leads to other symptoms, and you become mired in a cycle of symptoms and adjustments. This doesn't mean that the information in the Long Book is incorrect. It is just that the information in the Long Book is focused only on a limited area, correcting the symptom, the immediate problem. It does not look at the long term.

In contrast, the Short Book relates the problem the individual is encountering to a larger perspective: the entire movement pattern. The Short Book goes directly to the cause. The elimination of the symptom is a by-product of solving the larger movement concern.

Eliminating the cause is a long-term solution. Although the Short Book is shorter, the process might take a bit longer than the quick fix of the Long Book.

Mistakes

Sometimes it is necessary to draw attention to a problem, to delve into the how-not-to information. When we do, I feel that it is important that I present this information as observations rather than judgments. Judgments and labels don't provide performers with information that they can work with. Though it may be true, the judgment or label is useless information. It will usually cause the student to feel wrong and frustrated.

Constantin Stanislavski, perhaps the most famous of all acting teachers, expressed it this way: "There are actors who are mortally afraid of making mistakes. And this is always apparent on their faces because they go through their roles extraordinarily cautiously. A timid actor needs only to make a tiny slip and he is already lost" (Stanislavski and Pavel Rumyantsev, *Stanislavski on Opera*).

Judgment

The information in the Short Book does provide students with specific information that they can work with. It avoids judgments of right or wrong. This empowers the creative artist. Here is Stanislavski again on the subject: "You lost your head out of fear of being criticized, a feeling that is still inside you. The kind of self-criticism you need is the kind that ferrets out what is untrue in order to let you create what is true . . . The capacity to see what is good, what is beautiful, is a necessary part of an actor" (Stanislavski and Pavel Rumyantsev, *Stanislavski on Opera*).

Using This Book

This book is for performers striving toward maximum creative expression, trying to get the best results for the effort expended. You obviously don't need to know any of this unless you want to become a more skilled performer.

If becoming more skilled is your goal, this book deals with what is essential for you to connect with your physical instrument—your body and its components.

It will provide you with a language for discussing expression and movement.

The intent is to expand your potential for creative expression, to help you understand your physical instrument: what facilitates expression and what blocks it. The information is straightforward. However, the ideas are not linear. Every idea or concept affects, informs, and is in relation to every other topic or consideration. All of this is happening simultaneously.

Sometimes ideas and concepts are repeated in this book because they inform a later chapter or idea. This repetition allows the reader to consider the previously made points in relation to this new context. This referential quality is unavoidable. So think of it as a reminder.

Eventually it becomes clear that this interweaving of ideas results from the fact that the concepts on which the book is based are so closely interconnected.

Try not to judge yourself while working. Moving or posture is not about being wrong or right. It is a simple matter of efficiency. It's not that you are wrong; it's just that there is an easier way. If you know about the easier way, you have a choice.

Your instrument is your body. Your art, discipline, sport, or other pursuit may or may not require you to hold a musical instrument or tool in your hands; but whatever art or activity you are pursuing, a response is evoked in your body. In this way, your body is like the resonator for a musical instrument. How can we realistically expect to move forward if we don't have an awareness of our bodies and have them tuned for maximum expression?

In parts of the book are Awareness Studies and Awareness Tools. Awareness Studies are exercises designed to make you more conscious of habitual and inefficient ways that you move and to introduce you to steps you can take to allow more efficient movement patterns throughout your body. Awareness Tools are brief discussions of ways you can increase your perception that "everything is moving" as you put what you learn from this book into practice.

Think of the Awareness Studies and Awareness Tools as movement experiments. What results from trying a new movement experiment (as stated in the text) typically occurs for about 90 percent of the readers (or my class) at any given time. A particular observation may or may not be your experience. Because I am not working with you directly, I have no means of selecting what idea is most important to you at this particular time or of knowing if it is even necessary to present a particular idea to you.

This book describes my movement and performance theories in as logical a progression as possible considering the simultaneity of the subject material and interrelatedness of the ideas. The big picture is presented with the expectation that readers will see the usefulness of some ideas and concepts.

Some of these exercises will work for you; others might not quite. It's okay if you don't experience a change. This is a book. If I were coaching you, we'd find what part of this exploration isn't connecting with you, and you'd probably get the point and experience the difference right away.

If you don't experience/notice a change immediately, well, there's only so much one can gain from reading about movement. However, even if you don't experience the specific physical sensation (more freedom of movement or a release of tension) being demonstrated in an exercise, you most likely will be able to grasp the concept, premise, or overriding idea behind the exercise. That's enough for now.

Movement is an art and a science.

The anatomy information presented here is, to the best of my knowledge, true. I am a movement artist. I am not a movement scientist. Fortunately for me, I have friends who are. In many cases, I am relating and using the science metaphorically. This is how it should be taken.

Last, have fun with this stuff. Perhaps read the entire book quickly, and then go back to the beginning and start to reread and sort it out. That way you'll have the big picture as you begin. After all, that's what I had when I started writing it.

An overture is intended to introduce the major themes of a musical work, to be a first step. In the next section, I use a literary/pictorial overture to introduce the themes of this book to you. This might be the first time you have considered these themes or the subject of how your body affects your creative expression. The subject might, at first, seem unfamiliar. But it is not. The pictures are from life. There is no mystery to this study; it is happening all around us. All we have to do is be able to see the obvious.

Off you go.

Overture

In this picture of a mother and daughter working/playing together, you see a scene that could have taken place anywhere in America—or anywhere in the world for that matter. You look at it, and you think nothing of it.

However, by isolating the head and neck of the mother and comparing it to the head and neck of the daughter, you see two different pictures.

You can think about posture differently when you can see it differently. These photos help demonstrate the difference between balance and imbalance.

The mother's head is in front of her torso and is held forward of balance, while the child's head is balancing over and being supported by her torso.

It is important to point out that the child is not consciously aligning herself. Her posture is simply how it is: a natural, dynamic design; a pattern for efficient movement.

Observe how, in this photo by documentary photographer Dorothea Lange, the woman's head (which weighs about ten pounds or about 8 percent of the whole body mass) is also forward, out of balance. More muscular effort is required for the woman to support her head in such a configuration. Consequently, the rest of her body must compensate for this imbalance. For instance, her pelvis also comes forward as her shoulders go back. Muscles that normally would be involved in movement are engaged in maintaining the imbalance.

When the muscles tighten to maintain imbalance, their range of motion is restricted. Muscles that normally would be part of a larger movement pattern are now limited and no longer available to accompany, let's say, a gesture.

The result of this imbalance is that the woman's natural pattern for movement becomes distorted. Over the course of her day, a lot of energy is wasted.

The posture of the woman in the photo is less efficient than the child's balanced pattern shown in the preceding mother/daughter pictures. In the child's posture, you see a pattern that is supporting itself, is more efficient, and is more available for expression.

When a newborn is lying on the floor wiggling, it is actually strengthening the torso muscles that will one day create the spinal curves that will eventually allow the spine to support the weight of the body. After that, the baby's job is to develop the most efficient patterns for movement.

When my daughter was learning to stand, she would first put her forehead on the ground; then she lifted her derriere; and finally she would stand. This method lasted only a couple of days before she found an easier way to stand up. She wasn't doing it consciously; she was simply learning to move.

I'm sure the baby in the picture is not thinking about alignment. This baby, like all of us as babies, is ready to live, to explore and communicate with the world.

Intuitively we appreciate good posture; it is timeless. We see it in classic statuary and drawings like this study made by Italian Renaissance artist Michelangelo for his painting of the Libyan Sybil.

We all can recognize the wonderful interplay of the muscles. Aesthetically, we find good posture attractive. We call it grace or poise. With good posture, everyone appears—and is—more vital. Plus, as we perform with good posture, we feel better. We recognize good posture instinctively in gifted athletes and artists.

Great performers are first and foremost good movers.

Whether at work or at play, the child in this drawing has retained his natural movement pattern. The child carrying the chair allows the weight of the chair to be transferred from the top of the head, through the torso, legs, and feet, to the ground.

Like this child's body, your body is meant to use its weight to your advantage and to retain its natural alignment as you move. It will if you let it.

Equestrians have a term for when their animals retain their volume as they move (i.e., when they don't slump or compress). They call it *suspension*.

You can see an example of suspension in the study of a horse, drawn in the manner of Leonardo da Vinci's studies for the Trivulzio Monument. Da Vinci, widely considered to be one of the most diversely talented people who ever lived, was renowned as a painter and sculptor.

In the picture of the child playing, the child has retained his suspension. This is nothing done consciously; he just moves that way because that's how he's designed to move.

In the Lange photo of the woman standing with her head thrust forward, the woman is tightening and compressing her body. This loss of volume (decreased suspension) makes every movement more difficult and less efficient.

Suspension is dynamic, since we are always breathing and moving. With every breath and every movement, your spine is constantly contracting and expanding. Suspension is not a fixed volume or shape.

When you are under stress or you are trying to do a good job, the strategy that you might choose to help you feel in control of the situation is to tighten up your body and limit motion, as the children in these drawings are doing.

When you tighten the surface of your body (make it taut), you cause compression and lose suspension.

Because of the loss of suspension, muscles that are normally free to flow now bump up against each other. There just isn't as much room.

Consequently your coordination suffers, and every activity that you do becomes more difficult and requires more muscular effort.

The older children in these illustrations no longer have the natural, dynamic balance of the child with the chair. You can see how the pattern of imbalance and stress is evident in the bodies of the children pictured here.

These children have limited their capacity for expression without even knowing it.

Just as the forces of wind and rain sculpt our environment, movement patterns become etched on our bodies. Can you see how the posture of the woman in this picture reflects years of imbalance and compression?

Muscles that need to work constantly to compensate for imbalance become larger, and muscles not used wither and atrophy. The patterns we've developed linger and become recognizable to others as how we look, walk, and move—or "how we hold ourselves." Over time, the way you move determines how you look.

How you move becomes how you perform.

This picture reminds us that there is no escaping how you move.

Most of us can think of times when we've recognized someone from a distance simply by their posture—how they moved or held themselves.

For the performer, this recognizable pattern is part of every performance—every note played, every gesture, every word spoken or sung. For the athlete, the pattern is part of every effort and every movement.

In acting classes, we see these patterns all the time. Students often comment, for example, "This is how Mary/Alex acts." If your posture and movement patterns do not allow your whole body to be available to your intention, they limit your performance.

The man in this sketch is making an attempt at "good" posture.

My beginning students make similar attempts once they realize they have developed inefficient and counterproductive posture and movement habits.

The question becomes, "How do I change?" My students initially react by trying to find the perfect position, the correct position. The position that reflects how you think you are supposed to look, how you are supposed to "hold yourself" if you want to be right.

But it doesn't work.

By putting yourself into a position, all you do is interfere with the coordination of your body and decrease your capacity for expression. It doesn't matter if you are holding your body in a slump or in an attempt to stand up straight; compression is compression.

You might look a little better if you stand up straight. But, all in all, compression and holding are limiting. Good posture is dynamic and means being available to balance. Good posture is a result of a dynamic body.

The solution is not to achieve a better *still* position. The way out of this pattern of imbalance is to *allow motion*.

Have you watched beginning performers or athletes preparing to perform? Often, the first thing they do is attempt to stop all movement in their bodies. The surface of their bodies becomes tight and compresses; it is taut. They become still, like the person in this picture.

Perhaps the performers and athletes feel that holding their bodies still helps with focus, keeps them safe, and ensures their success.

They aren't entirely wrong: unwanted motion can be distracting. But believe it or not, unwanted motion is actually the result of lack of movement in the entire body.

I demonstrate this when I work with conductors. They are always amazed at how much more refined the gesture is and how much more expressive the body is when more of the body moves.

For some reason, we equate stillness with being better, more correct. But what has more capacity for expression: stillness or motion?

Expression is motion.

Compression causes imbalance and limits movement. You can see the woman in this illustration focusing intently on her work. She is living in her head, and her body becomes still. Her forward focus causes compression on the front of her torso as her head comes forward to her work.

There are psychological payoffs to holding yourself still: it might make you feel like you are doing a good job, or, like the young man in the illustration, it might make you feel that you look cool or that you fit in.

That is why adequate preparation of your material and knowing how to work are so important. Once you know your lines or music, you are free to play. If you are trying to remember what comes next, expression isn't even a consideration.

Look at the referee in this illustration.

Is the referee tense in order to do his job better, to make himself feel that he will do his job better, or to show the crowd that he is working and on top of the situation?

Whatever his reason, his habit of tension has not contributed to his performance and may even be causing him pain.

The child in this picture illustrates how we are designed to sit. The woman is straining, trying to show her intention, her enthusiasm.

The child is not thinking about how to sit, yet his body has retained suspension and is balancing effortlessly. His body is available to express his intention without effort. He is just doing it.

This drawing of a child speaks volumes about posture.

It could be captioned, "The performing artist's body, vital and alive, capable of communicating the subtlest nuance to our fellow human beings."

Again we return to the photograph of the mother and daughter.

Do you still look at it and think nothing of it? Or are you now better able to see the difference between the two figures?

In your own life, when you know what you are doing and what is possible, you will have a choice. If you are unaware of your habits and how they relate to performance, it is very difficult to grow in your art.

Where there is perhaps a province in which the photograph can tell us nothing more than what we see with our own eyes, there is another in which it proves to us how little our eyes permit us to see.

—DOROTHEA LANGE

These pictures are examples of posture and expression in everyday life. Perhaps you can see the head and neck relationships and resultant patterns of tension.

To become different from what we are, we must have some awareness of what we are.

—ZEN SAYING

Part One

The Capacity for Expression

Anyone who has never made
a mistake has never tried
anything new.

—ALBERT EINSTEIN

Chapter 1
A First Step

You cannot at the very beginning of our work, have any conception of the evil that results from muscular spasms and physical contraction.

—CONSTANTIN STANISLAVSKI, *An Actor Prepares*

The story is told that in the ancient theaters of Greece, large vessels were placed in the aisles so that they might resonate with the performance, the words, and the ideas of the playwright. The intention was that the urns might send these vibrations—the universal truths of humankind—into the heavenly spheres (the cosmos).

Having spent most of my adult years involved in the puzzle that is the theater, I found this concept most clearly illustrated to me while coaching symphonic and wind conductors.

Standing in front of the orchestra, next to the conductor, I was viscerally connected to the sound. In that moment, I realized that the first job, the primary responsibility, of the conductor is to resonate with the music—its vibrations, sound, mood, tone, and timbre—and then figuratively "conduct it to the spheres." We performers are the urn.

This book is about the process of allowing and "resonating with." Your craft/medium/art directs these vibrations or *intentions.*

The journey you will take as you read this book will lead you to a level of performance where you are experiencing and resonating with what you are doing while you are doing it.

Exclude/Include

I'm convinced that the common factor at the core of movement and/or performance problems is that the performer is excluding something: for example, your thought process excludes some possibility for movement, or your movement pattern excludes certain muscles or joints. All obstacles to performing stem from this tendency to *exclude.* If this is true, then the strategy for success is to *include.*

This means that you allow more possibilities. When you understand how you move and when you include all muscles and joints as you move, your entire body is available for expression.

Implied Limitations

Assumptions about how you move, either conscious or unconscious, influence how you move. You may be restricting your capacity for physical expression unknowingly, restraining yourself unnecessarily—imposing implied limitations.

Once you are aware of the limitations you impose on yourself through habit or as a result of misunderstanding how the body moves, it's really not too difficult to understand how to achieve greater flow and balance in your movements.

Physical Limitations

Here's an example of how our assumptions can manifest themselves as physical limitations.

Suppose I ask you to stand up and look to the right. Like most people, you will probably turn only your head to the right. Not because of a true physical limitation on your movement, but because of an unconscious implied limitation.

What you are not aware of is that in order to turn just your head to the right, you have to hold the rest of your body still. That unconscious stillness has blocked your capacity to be expressive.

When I ask my students to look to the right, the movement usually looks like the illustration on the lower left.

The second drawing shows the full range of movement possible for someone when turning to the right while *not* constrained by implied limitations (i.e., boundaries on how he or she perceives or interprets "looking to the right").

In neither instance has the student moved her feet.

The difference between the two movements for looking right is that the movement *on the right* avoids holding still and uses more of the body than the movement shown in the first drawing.

The more of your body that is involved in a movement or gesture, the greater are your range of movement and your capacity for expression.

We also impose mental limitations on ourselves. If we want to improve our capacity for expression, we need to think differently. We commonly refer to this as "thinking outside the box."

THE NINE-DOT PUZZLE

Here's a puzzle that illustrates mental limitations.

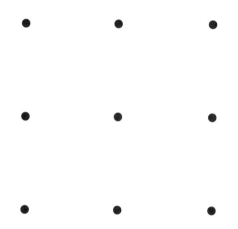

Draw four continuous straight lines (without lifting the pen) so that each of the nine dots has at least one line running through it.

The only way to connect the nine dots as required is to allow the lines to extend beyond the confines of the box—to think beyond the implied limitation. To trace the solution here, start at the dot in the lower left corner and follow the arrows to connect all the dots, ending at the top right dot.

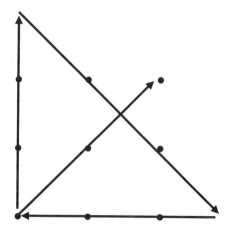

You can understand how this concept works in your body when you consider what I've already said about the implied limitations a person might impose on himself or herself when asked to make a simple movement, such as looking to the right.

It is our implied physical and mental limitations, conscious and unconscious, that hold us back.

Getting There

Performing "correctly" becomes a problem for beginners because there is so much new information to juggle. There are too many individual points to think about at any given time.

Eventually, through experience, we forget about the individual points. We learn that the key, as the old Nike commercial suggests, is to "just do it"—which to me means being available to move without censoring one's intention. The process of getting to this point is what is known as the *artistic struggle*.

By comparison, being a starving artist is relatively easy. We know how to fix that: we can get a sandwich. We don't even know the process involved in solving the *artistic struggle*.

Getting to the point of pure intention and unfettered expression involves changing your understanding of how you move, your vocabulary, your aesthetic, your thought process, and habitual movement patterns that you don't even know you have. All of these elements affect your ability to increase your capacity for expression.

Everything Is Moving

This isn't rocket science. It's common knowledge that everything is moving.

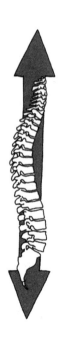

Posture is the position of a person's body while standing or sitting. Posture is determined by the person's ability to maintain balance against the force of gravity, which constantly pulls the body downward. The action of certain muscles keeps the body upright. These muscles include those that keep the back, hips, and knees from bending. Because of the constant give and take of the pull of gravity and of muscle action, posture is a dynamic, ever-changing state. It is impossible for a person to stand perfectly still, because there is always some degree of sway. If postural control is inadequate, the sway becomes excess and the person loses balance.

Good posture requires the least amount of muscle activity to breathe well and to maintain an upright position.

— *World Book Encyclopedia*

With every breath and every move, your spine is expanding or contracting.

Dr. Ida Rolf was a biochemist who developed a system of soft tissue manipulation and movement education that organized the whole body in gravity. Her system of structural integration is known as "Rolfing." In her book *Rolfing: Reestablishing the Natural Alignment and Structural Integration of the Human Body for Vitality and Well-Being*, she states, "Contrary to the general idea, normal respiration in a balanced body involves movement not merely in the thorax, but from the sacrum all the way up to the cranium. In normal inspiration, the spine lengthens from one end to the other; in expiration, the spine shortens."

This ebb and flow of life creates movement and a pumping action throughout the entire body. As you breathe, your body is balancing and counterbalancing in relation to this process. Breathing is therefore a process that involves the whole body, from the top of your head to the soles of your feet. You are in constant motion. This pumping action is an aid to circulation. Your whole body is a pump. Your heart, of course, is the primary pump, and then your legs. Finally, every movement that you make is part of the pumping action of the body.

As you breathe, your spine is designed to lengthen with the inhalation and shorten with the exhalation.

Ideally, every time you move, there will also be a corresponding lengthening and/or contraction of the spine. Think about it: you're always breathing. So unless you are holding your breath, there will be movement of the spine.

As you breathe and as you move, your spine is designed to be available to lengthen and contract in relation to your intention and to the corresponding movement. It is probably safe to surmise, then, that your breath and your intention to move are indisputably linked.

As an ancillary benefit, if you can allow this movement of the spine to be unencumbered, every movement that you make will consequently feel lighter and be easier. It is wasted effort to hold your breath or hold your spine still, since doing so makes it a lot harder to breathe.

Here's the deal: the torso (the human body with the exception of the head and limbs), when combined with the head and neck, is the most expressive part of your body. If you allow your head and torso to move when you perform, the movement of the spinal column will contribute substantially to the overall expressiveness of your body by amplifying your gestures. Allowing the spine to expand and contract as you breathe and move is what makes your performance magical.

Isn't it ironic that when, in fact, everything is moving, we usually attempt to solve our movement/performance problems with stillness?

Chapter 2
The Components of Movement: Balance, Force, Flow, Mind

Learning how to move the limbs and trunk with unaffected elegance and awareness ought to be the first element in the training of an actor.

—DARIO FO, *The Tricks of the Trade*

Every movement you make can be thought of as a combination of three physical dynamics: balance, muscular force (or energy), and flow.

Although we will consider them separately, these physical components are inseparable and mutually interdependent. Balance cannot exist without force and flow, there is no flow without force and balance, and force depends on balance and flow. They exist simultaneously.

The quality of the interplay between these three dynamics determines the efficiency or inefficiency of how you move. As the efficiency of your movement increases, so does your capacity for expression.

The fourth component, which is nonphysical and influences every movement that you make, is your mind. How you think your body moves and what you think you have to do to move it affect how you move. Thought is the element that can most quickly change your movement patterns, but it may be the hardest element for you to change.

The mind governs the physical dynamics and can cause us to revert to familiar patterns. Conversely, pure unfettered intention is our most powerful tool. It is our intention, expressed through our bodies, that allows us to communicate with our fellow humans.

Not only must the body be kept supple and agile, so must the mind.

—SIR LAURENCE OLIVIER, *On Acting*

Component One: Balance

The body is designed for movement. When you move, your body is meant to be in balance. You are constantly in the process of balancing and counterbalancing weight shifts in relation to even the smallest movement.

The principal problem that blocks physical performance is that people don't allow counterbalance to happen.

The Line of Balance

For the human body, the line of balance is a line drawn vertically through the body, as shown in these illustrations.

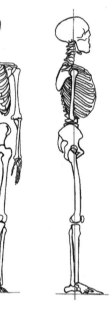

Your support is organized around the line of balance, and your weight is transferred through the center of the body.

As shown in the side view, the line of balance passes through the ankle, the knee, the hip joint, the body's center of gravity (the point at which the average weight of the body is centered, located at sacral vertebra 2), the shoulder, and the atlanto-occipital joint (where your head attaches on top of your spine).

This is the proper interrelationship of the body's articulating surfaces for optimal balance and distribution of weight when standing. Any weight shift forward will cause an opposite counterbalancing movement to the back. A movement to the right means something must move to the left. You balance around the line of balance.

Notice, in the front view, that the line of balance falls between the legs. You are balanced between the legs. The line of balance is dynamic. This is important!

In real life, you are rarely straight. You are far more likely to be spiraled, bent, rotated, and so on.

Oppositional Movements and Counterbalance

For every directional movement you make, there must be a complementary opposite movement (a counterbalancing movement) if you want to maintain balance without tension.

Counterbalancing is the act of offsetting a movement (or a weight or force) with an equal movement (weight or force). Opposition is the physical movement that allows counterbalance to occur.

Think about it: when you run, your right arm goes forward as your left arm goes back. That's an example of oppositional movements (one forward, one back), with the result being that the arm going forward counterbalances the arm going back.

A principal cause of most physical tension is nothing more than not letting this opposition and counterbalance occur.

PICKING UP KEYS

A good example of how tension is created when opposition is restricted is the movement people make when picking up an object lying on the ground.

Working with performers or others wanting to improve their performance technique (e.g., instrumentalists, yoga practitioners, horseback riders), I'll sometimes drop a set of keys on the floor and then ask them to pick up the keys. They bend from the waist and reach out with one hand, as shown in this illustration.

Contrast this illustration with the following one.

In this second drawing, the model is using the movement pattern that a small child would use. A child allows his or her entire body to get into the act. The child reaches down for the object with one hand and allows the opposite hand to counterbalance the movement.

Try this for yourself. Try it both ways. Isn't it amazing how much easier it is when, like the child, you allow counterbalance?

You can often see counterbalance in action if you watch a golf tournament. As professional golfers reach into the cup to retrieve a ball, they lift one leg to counterbalance this move.

The Line of Balance Is Moving

What happens when you shake someone's hand with your right hand, but the oppositional movement doesn't seem to involve the left arm? Where's the counterbalance?

SHAKING HANDS

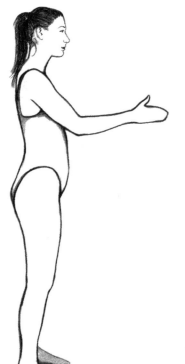

In a movement like shaking hands, the oppositional movement occurs in the torso and the entire body. The line of balance shifts more toward one leg than the other. The movement of the torso offsets the weight shift of the right arm reaching forward.

So the oppositional movement does involve the other arm after all.

It is just that your left arm is not involved directly in the counterbalancing movement. It is simply hanging there, attached to the body, and as your body moves, so does your left arm. But the weight of your left arm, no matter where it is, still affects the counterbalance.

Shaking hands implies moving only one arm. Right there is the problem. You can't move only one arm. We assume, because we have never thought about it, that we are moving only one arm, but, in fact, we are moving the entire body. Moving your arm to shake hands or pick up keys also involves the moving line of balance.

Dynamic Balance vs. Static Imbalance

Balance is dynamic, and imbalance is static. When we try to achieve balance without a counterbalancing movement, we end up in a state of imbalance.

A student once asked me, "What do you mean we are out of balance? We don't fall over." And he's right: we don't fall over. But the extra effort involved in maintaining imbalance blocks expression. I explained to him that balance is dynamic while imbalance is static.

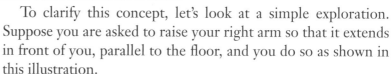

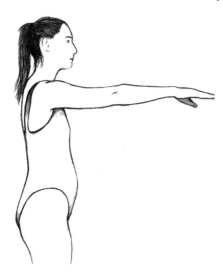

To clarify this concept, let's look at a simple exploration. Suppose you are asked to raise your right arm so that it extends in front of you, parallel to the floor, and you do so as shown in this illustration.

This kind of movement is what I call *static imbalance*. Instead of allowing the entire body to counterbalance naturally, you are holding the body still (static) and using more force to move only the arm (implied limitation) and nothing else.

When you move with static imbalance, you use only the shoulder joint. You tighten the rest of your body that would normally move to counterbalance and/or accompany the motion of raising the arm; that is, you make the muscles and joints taut or rigid. There is no flow. There is no dynamic balance. There is only force in the form of the extra work.

Static imbalance limits your ability to perform physical activity. If you are a performing artist, it shuts down your capacity for expression. To achieve dynamic balance, you must allow the shift in weight to be counterbalanced.

In the first illustration here, the arm is extended in static imbalance. Compare this movement to the second illustration where more of the model's body is involved in the movement of extending the arm, allowing the body to balance and counterbalance dynamically. Instead of holding the torso still, the model allows the movement to involve the entire body. The movement shown is more complex, since it uses more joints. *The more joints involved, the more expressive the movement is.*

Balance (dynamic) requires less effort than imbalance (static). Dynamic balance is more efficient. The muscles and joints are free to relate to the movement of the rest of the body, so you are able to maintain flow and an economy of force. *When more of your body is available to the movement, your capacity for expression increases.*

Look at this simple movement and analyze how you might allow counterbalancing to occur so that you don't limit yourself to a static response.

This illustration shows a female model standing with her arms at her sides. The model's posture reflects the weight of the arms being at the sides.

As we've just discussed, the moment the model extends an arm in front, as in the next illustration, the weight distribution of the body changes.

Try this for yourself.

1. Stand up and raise an arm.

   Your entire body must reconfigure to accommodate this weight shift, and it will if you let it. You now have a choice between static imbalance and allowing dynamic balance.

   Now, just like picking up the keys, you want to allow counterbalance.

2. This time, as you raise your arm, let your opposite shoulder go back, and at the same time, let your body move instead of holding it still and tight, with muscles taut.
3. Notice that the movement is easier. Also notice that your torso is now involved in the movement.

   This movement is now perhaps more expressive than your first attempt. In fact, if you don't tighten up in the first place, all of this might just happen on its own. There is no need to consciously move the other shoulder. You don't have to *make* your body counterbalance. It comes naturally.

   Your job is to *allow* counterbalance to occur.

Balancing

In graduate school, beloved acting teacher Arthur Wagner required us to express our actions as gerunds (verbs ending in *-ing*), in order that our actions be thought of as active. Perhaps *balancing* is an even better word choice here than *balance*, because it implies a constantly moving process. So it is with balance and the body. The process of balancing is dynamic.

Component Two: Force

There is an appropriate amount of force (muscular energy) required to maintain balance and flow plus breathing and locomotion.

Imbalance Requires Excess Force

It takes more work (force) to hold your body still and out of balance than to allow it to be in balance. It takes more energy to keep parts of your body from moving. It takes extra force to prevent your body from naturally counterbalancing. What we are after is an economy of force.

This illustration (which we've examined before) is an example of a pattern of compensation and stillness. You can observe the head being held forward out of balance, using excess force and limiting flow.

I've already noted that the head weighs about ten pounds. Next time you are in the grocery store, pick up a couple of five-pound bags of flour: that's roughly what your head weighs. Think how much force (energy) is wasted when the head is held out of balance all day.

Unfortunately, we have no sense of the weight of our bodies when we move. So we don't appreciate how much force we're expending to hold that weight out of balance.

Economy of Force vs. Excess Effort or Tension

When I talk about force, I'm talking about the appropriate amount of energy required to maintain dynamic balance and balanced activity. In reality, most people use far more energy than they need to as they go about their daily activities. Notice the man in this illustration.

When muscles of the neck and shoulder are busy holding your head out of balance, they are not as available to flow with the change in weight involved in a gesture such as moving your arm. You are impeding flow, and consequently you are in your own way.

I have come to think that a lot of tension is nothing more than the trapping of this counterbalancing motion.

Returning to the example of holding the arm in front of the torso (shown again in this illustration), note that it takes more force *not* to let the opposite shoulder (and the rest of the body) counterbalance the movement of the arm in front of the torso.

Any activity (e.g., conducting, dancing, kicking a soccer ball, martial arts, tai chi) requires less muscular force when performed in balance than when performed out of balance.

It is noteworthy that the more efficient your movement becomes, the less you feel the work you are doing. After a successful theater or musical performance or movement class, such as yoga, I often hear a performer comment, "It didn't feel like I was doing anything."

Tension, imbalance, overwork, and trying hard are the enemies of effective and inspired performance.

Excess Force Does Not Equal Control

Overcontrol (excess force) impedes our ability to balance and destroys flow. Efficient movement doesn't mean that muscles don't work: it simply means that muscles don't *over*work.

You often see excess force used by beginners in any discipline—the arts or sports or other fields. Beginners go through all sorts of tension patterns, while the more experienced simply "do it." For most people, this pattern of overcontrol becomes so ingrained that they don't even know they're doing it. For many, it's a problem that may result in injury.

One of the first steps toward change is simply to become aware of how much force you are using and how much force you need.

When you rid yourself of excess force, more of your body moves. Your capacity for expression increases, and consequently your performance will improve.

An economy of force increases our capacity for expression, because it makes more of our life energy available and causes us to waste less energy in performance.

Component Three: Flow

Every movement you make flows through the entire body, as it constantly balances and counterbalances shifts in weight with an economy of muscular force. Stanislavski put it well: "As long as you have physical tenseness you cannot even think about delicate shadings of feeling or the spiritual life of your part. Consequently, before you attempt to create anything it is necessary for you to get your muscles in proper condition, so that they do not impede your actions" (*An Actor Prepares*).

As demonstrated in chapter 1 in the illustrated examples of a young woman looking to the right, you do not have to let your thoughts and assumptions limit you. Looking to the right with the whole body involves more than the head and neck; the movement also flows through the shoulders, torso, hips, knees, ankles, and feet. It is a more complex movement.

A skilled performer (e.g., actor, musician, or athlete) has more of his or her body involved and flowing in the activity. Therefore, instead of the body being held still, the torso is engaged and is part of the expressive flow pattern.

Performers: Unskilled/Skilled

One of the differences between the skilled performer and the unskilled performer of any activity is the degree of freedom in the performer's body.

For many unskilled performers, there is so much to think about when preparing to perform (e.g., play an instrument, hit a golf ball, conduct a symphony) that the beginning tendency is to stiffen the joints—to unconsciously stop movement. In other words, the unskilled performer typically begins with tension and compression, so he or she can concentrate on other aspects of the performance.

Although you initially think this stiffening/tightening strategy will help, very soon it becomes the problem that is holding you back. It is very important for performers and their coaches to recognize this fact. It is also very important not to demand success too quickly.

Skilled performers are capable of more complex movement patterns because they are not locking joints with excess muscular effort in order to perform. More joints are available to move, to express intention. It is as if the person has only one joint, defined as the entire body moving as one.

The audience recognizes this superior skill instantly. They also can sense (perhaps only subliminally) when it is not happening.

Fortunately, it is possible to learn and to teach how you can use more of your body when you perform. Whether you are dancing, acting, conducting, practicing yoga, giving a business presentation, or playing a sport, this is the process that you will need to adopt if you want to become a more skilled performer.

Whole-Body Movement

The fundamental for healthy and efficient movement is that the whole body moves as one in support of your intention. This could be a definition of flow.

You are wrapped around a breath. Your body expands and contracts as you move. Every movement is in relation to your entire body. Coordinated movement uses the entire body, as it balances and counterbalances with an economy of effort.

Whole-body movement (an Alexander Technique concept), moving like a string of pearls (the tai chi version), is what we are striving for.

When you move, everything moves!

PATTERNS VS. PARTS

The body moves in patterns rather than parts.

Although any movement you make flows through the entire body, most of us conceive of our bodies as moving in parts. If you move in parts, you must hold one part in order to move another part, then hold "this" part to move "that" part again.

Moving in parts is an inefficient way to move. It is sequential rather than simultaneous. It is more efficient and more expressive to allow all joints to be available to any change in weight as you move.

When you're moving in a relaxed and balanced way, your entire body moves as one. You don't begin to walk by holding your breath and moving only your leg; ideally your entire body expands into motion.

You can see what happens when a student is asked to reach to the right as far as possible. At first the arm moves alone; then the upper torso moves; and finally, with a little coaching, the left foot becomes engaged. In other words, the movement ultimately uses and flows through the whole body.

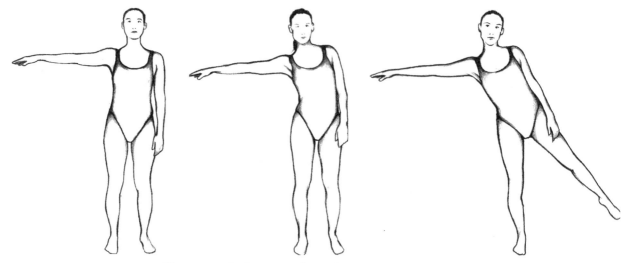

If you reach far enough with your arm, your opposite foot must move to counterbalance the arm's movement, or you will fall over.

Moving in parts is linked to how we all tend to conceptualize our bodies. We think, "This is where my arm is. This is the top half of my body." In later chapters, we'll redefine the body to reflect a more accurate and broader understanding of moving in patterns.

For demonstration purposes, the illustration above shows a large movement. But even if you made the movement smaller, as in the illustration on the left, it would still involve the foot. This is just a subtler movement and not as obvious.

The next time you shake someone's hand, remember that your feet and the rest of your body are also a part of that movement pattern.

You don't have to hold your breath, tighten the surface of your body, become rigid, make your muscles taut, hold yourself still, or move anything consciously. You just have to allow your entire body to be part of the movement. Simply shake the person's hand.

If you were standing while reading this book and turned the page, the act of turning the page would, if allowed, subtly flow through your foot. The movement wouldn't be as extreme as in the earlier example of reaching to the right, but there would still be flow.

Your whole body is designed to work with all the parts integrated and functioning simultaneously. With every breath and every movement, your spine is designed to be expanding and contracting. This is a recurring theme of this book.

Your body has more than six hundred muscles, 206 bones, and around 190 movable and semimovable joints (depending on how you count). That's almost a thousand body parts to consciously keep track of and get right when you move. But we don't need to keep track.

All these muscles, bones, and joints are designed to work together, balancing and counterbalancing, with the muscles free to expand and contract and with the joints available to move with the subtlest shifts of weight, in response to your intention.

All great performers have this flow.

Component Four: Mind

Thought is the nonphysical component of motion. Your understanding of movement (assumptions as well as fundamentals) affects the *quality* of your movement.

> Thoughts are embodied in acts, and a man's actions in turn affect his mind. His mind affects his body and again his body, or its condition, has its reflex action on his mind. You must learn how to rest your body, free your muscles and, at the same time, your psyche.
>
> —CONSTANTIN STANISLAVSKI, IN STANISLAVSKI AND PAVEL RUMYANTSEV, *Stanislavski on Opera*

While balance, force, and flow are the physical components of motion, the nonphysical component, your thinking, affects every movement that you make. Your mind has the power to override balance, force, and flow (i.e., the power of mind over matter).

It is the assumptions you make that inform and/or limit your movement patterns.

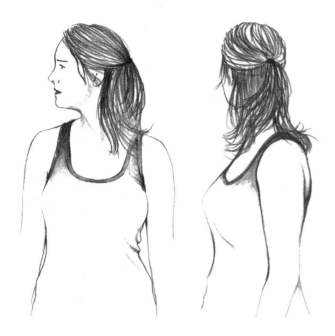

In these illustrations from the discussion in chapter 1 about implied limitations, the female model looks to the right first by moving just the head and then by using the entire body. The implied limitation that she accepts in the first instance (that only the head turns to look to the right) noticeably limits her movement.

Mind Over Matter

The mind of a child has no preconceptions about the body's limitations. His or her movements reflect a sense of freedom. As we get older, our movements are informed by any implied limitations we accept as true. Again, it's mind over matter.

What stops the counterbalancing from happening? What causes our natural movement pattern to be interrupted? What thoughts, belief systems, myths, or unconscious habits cause us to tighten up, compress, hold our breath, and limit ourselves?

It is our thinking, conscious and unconscious, that influences everything we do. It is simply mind over matter.

Intention

Intention is the determination to act in a certain way. When you intend to do something, you have it in mind as a purpose or goal. This is true whether we are talking about day-to-day activities or about a performer's intention on stage.

English writer and intellectual Aldous Huxley, in his book *The Art of Seeing*, identifies the two things that get in the way of pure intention: fear of failure and wanting to do a good job. Stanislavski explains that fear of failure and wanting to do a good job are so dangerous for the actor because they are unactable and that even slight pressure somewhere within the body can arrest the creative faculty.

For the acting process to work, you must be doing something. The question is not "How do I say the line?" but "What am I doing? What is my intention?" If you do something as if you are really doing it, the process of doing it makes it real: you experience it. If you merely try to say a line of dialogue a certain way, this process of becoming real doesn't happen, because you are not experiencing it. Instead, you are only experiencing saying the line a certain way.

For the musician, dancer, singer, or any performing artist or athlete, it is the same: you must experience what you are doing. Fear of failure and wanting to do a good job exist in the mind. Fear and trying take you out of the moment and distract you from your intention.

INTENTION AND NEURONS

Why does intention work? Thoughts trigger a physiological response in the body. As a result, an interesting thing happens when you visualize yourself doing an activity: the body's neurons fire just as they would if you were actually doing the activity. So in a sense, as far as the body is concerned, visualizing and doing are the same.

I once was watching Olympic high jumpers on television. Before the male athlete jumped, I could see him visualizing how he was going to address the jump. He was taking advantage of the fact that when you visualize an action, the neurons respond to your intention.

To me, this means that *what you are doing is what you are doing while you are doing it.*

If you are experiencing what you are doing, then the brain fires the neurons for experiencing what you are doing. If you are greeting someone, the neurons for greeting fire, and you experience greeting someone.

However, when you are judging yourself while you perform, then the neurons for judging yourself fire. If you are trying to do a good job, the neurons for trying to do a good job fire. If you are afraid of failure, the neurons for being afraid of failure fire.

In short, if you are judging yourself while you perform, that is what you are doing on stage: you are judging yourself. If you are re-creating a scene the same way you did it last time, that's what you are doing: re-creating. You are not, as they say, *in the moment*. Your neurons can't lie.

Now let us go back to pure intention, where you have the intention and act. You can be in the moment. You can be experiencing what you are doing; you can be connected. It works the same for singers, instrumentalists, and conductors.

The musician's job, for example, is to be available to the music as he or she works his or her way through the line—not ahead of it, not behind it, but performing in the moment. If musicians are judging themselves, they are not playing. They are judging themselves. I would rather hear them play.

Specificity   If your intent is undefined, your performance will be vague. This is why specificity of your intention is so important. Music, for example, doesn't simply "get louder"; it can "grow," "swell," "crest," and so on. "Growing" is more specific than merely "getting louder." The specificity of your action creates a richer moment because the neurons that are firing are more specific to your intention. "Getting louder" is a more general effect, so it is not as connected to you. You want to fire exactly the neurons that you want to be firing. Your intention will then be as clear as possible.

> We cannot know what you see in your imagination but we shall be drawn
> by your inner visions and we, the spectators, will paint in our imaginations
> our own pictures, under the impact of your creative inspiration.
>
> —CONSTANTIN STANISLAVSKI, IN STANISLAVSKI AND
> PAVEL RUMYANTSEV, *Stanislavski on Opera*

DYNAMIC INTENTION

Performing is a dynamic process of receiving impulses from our environment and then intentionally responding to those impulses. This could be the definition of the acting process.

We receive impulses through our senses. Our senses take in; they do not push out. We must be open to receiving impulses. This process of receiving impulses is blocked when you focus on yourself while performing: you are no longer available to receive impulses and resonate with them, because your intention is now directed toward dealing with fear of failure or wanting to do a good job, so the dynamic process becomes static.

Intention must be connected to what you are doing, not how you are doing it.

What we are after is pure dynamic intention. If you are available to pure intention, you don't really need to be concerned about how to move. Unfortunately, pure intention is also corrupted by both conscious and unconscious assumptions about how our bodies move. The ideal is to allow movement by eliminating inhibiting thought patterns. Pure intention makes freedom of expression possible.

The more of the performer's body that is available to his or her intention and the more specific that intention is, the greater is the performer's capacity for expression.

INTENTION AND MOVEMENT

The following formula illustrates how intention relates to movement.

1. *You have the intention to move.* Let's say you have the intention to reach for a latte.
2. *The joints are available.* Rather than tighten and become rigid, the joints and muscles become available for movement.

When I say that the joints are available, I am using shorthand for a larger concept: it is not just the joints but the whole body that must be available for movement. However, it is easier for students to conceptualize what is moving or not moving if they notice whether their joints are available—that is, whether their joints are being held or not.

3. *You follow the shift of weight.* As your arm moves forward toward the latte, oppositional movement occurs throughout the whole body to counterbalance the weight shift.

This process is instantaneous and simultaneous with your intention. It just happens. This is what I mean by happening "in the moment." You experience what you are doing *as* you do it.

Focus

The word *focus* is used to mean the center of attention or emphasis. When performers speak of focus, we mean directed attention. Your mind has the power to change your focus—to narrow, broaden, or split your directed attention. Let's consider some of the ways focus affects your movement, as well as how your thinking can influence your focus.

SINGULAR FOCUS

When you engage in an activity such as inserting your house key into the lock, you will usually focus on only a very small area—the keyhole. This singular focus on the keyhole is usually accompanied by a general tightening and stillness or tautness of the surface of the body. This tightening seems necessary to make sure that you hit the target.

A singular focus is a static focus (in one direction only) and doesn't allow for opposition and counterbalance.

To achieve "perfect posture," most people try to hold themselves up by pushing from the lower back, as shown in the illustration to the right. This doesn't work, because they are focusing on just one area to hold themselves up. This singular focus interrupts the coordination of the entire body and creates tension.

Let's try a brief exercise to illustrate how singular focus works.

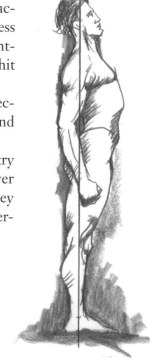

AWARENESS STUDY: Singular Focus

1. While sitting in a chair, sit "up straight."
2. Notice that you tightened your hip and thigh and maybe other areas in order to push yourself up. Usually, the pushing up is from a single spot in your back.

The tension in your hips/thighs is not really caused by a belief that you need to tense your thighs to sit up straight, and it's not just the result of a habit of holding yourself in a particular way. It's also the result of your single focus on your lower back. Any time you focus on a particular area, you'll most likely cause tension somewhere else—usually the surrounding or complementary muscles.

Focus and Muscular Discomfort   If I touch your arm with my finger, the only part of your body that you have awareness of at that moment is the spot that my finger is touching. You have a singular focus on the place I'm touching. I have noticed that people tend to "freeze" the muscles around my finger so they can better focus, in the same way that you tense your body for better focus while concentrating. This narrowing of focus and tensing of the body is all unconscious, of course.

A similar thing happens when you have a sore neck or shoulder. When you have a pain in your back, shoulder, and so on, the pain acts like my finger. It gives you a focal point, and the surrounding muscles tend to stop moving.

An application of the lesson we've learned about balance, effort (force), and entire body movement (flow) tells us that if you want to get rid of the ache, you must allow the area around the pain, as well as the rest of your body, to soften and move. Next time you get a minor ache, see if you can get more of your body moving. Most people notice that when they allow movement, the discomfort goes away sooner.

SOFT FOCUS

How many times have you heard the statement "Look at that"? This statement implies that you can go out and grab a glimpse of something. However, your eyes don't work that way. They don't radiate sight outward like a laser beam. They allow the image into your consciousness.

"Soft focus" means that instead of focusing on a particular point, you try to take in the whole. For example, while you focus on the keyhole, also allow the image of the door to enter your awareness. As soon as you expand your focus, your muscles will begin to relax, making you aware of how you have tightened them unnecessarily to focus on the keyhole.

This works with how you focus on your body as well. As I've noted, if you focus on one spot, the surrounding muscles tense. If you can expand your focus to encompass your whole body, the tensed muscles will relax. This softening of focus can be a valuable tool if you want to increase your capacity for expression.

For centuries, martial artists have used the idea of soft focus. If you have ever seen people doing tai chi, you will have noticed that the players usually do it in a group. To perform in a group, the individual must extend his focus to include the group, while being aware of himself. This is really a form of soft focus. When you work with yourself on your posture or while you are practicing your musical instrument, golfing, fly-fishing, and so on, try taking in the outside world. You'll be amazed at how helpful it is in allowing your muscles to relax and your movement to become easier.

The key word in the preceding discussion of soft focus is *while*. Allowing an expanded image in *while* focusing on your task can help you become aware of the amount of tension in your body.

To illustrate this idea, let's try a demonstration created by the Israeli movement specialist Moshé Feldenkrais.

AWARENESS STUDY: Allowing the Image In

1. Point at a corner of the room with one finger, and focus on that spot.
2. Notice that your body has tightened to facilitate your focus.
3. Now, while you are pointing at the corner, also take in as much of the room as possible.
4. Notice that as you allow the expanded image in, the tension in your body decreases, and you can feel your muscles soften.

TWO FOCI

Another way to avoid a singular focus is to have two focal points (two foci). An exercise that is helpful in showing the value of two foci uses the abdominal cavity and the head as focal points.

Here's how it works: I am working with you, and I stand facing you. I put my right hand out to shake your hand. As you put your hand forward to shake mine, the surface of your body becomes taut to accommodate this movement. (If you have trouble discerning this, bring your hand up as fast as you can.)

I then ask you to try it again with a split focus: put equal focus on your head and on your belly while you raise your arm. You comply, and immediately you relax a bit.

FOCUSING AHEAD OF THE MOMENT

When you rush, you are focusing on where you want to be or what you want to achieve instead of being where you are. All the rushing does is make you tense. Turn-of-the-century Australian movement teacher F. M. Alexander called this "end gaining."

If you put too much focus on where you are going (singular focus), you'll notice that your entire body is tightening with your focus and that you are losing sight of where you've been and where you are.

The following exercise allows you to experience the difference between being ahead of the moment and being present.

AWARENESS STUDY: "I'm There/I'm Here"

1. The first approach is to focus on where you are going. Pick out a spot on the floor ahead of you, and as you walk toward it, with every step, repeat to yourself, "I'm there, I'm there, I'm there."
2. The second approach is a practice in being present. Pick out a spot on the floor again, but this time repeat as you walk, "I'm here, I'm here, I'm here."

Being "there" or "here" relates to the concept of being "in the moment." To be in the moment, you have to know where you are going and be where you are. If your focus is on "here" (where you are now) while you are going "there," your body will be more present and available.

The Big Movement Myths

Famed director Peter Brook observed in his book *The Physical Life of the Actor*, "Standing still has to be the ultimate achievement of a body that can move, not the limitation of a body that can't do any better." It is important to understand how some of the assumptions that we have about moving our bodies are really false assumptions. In other words, it is habit and familiarity that have become the filter for new experience. What clouds this issue is that the movement myths we believe are based on how you *are* moving, not on how you are *able* to move. In a sense, they are true, because they are accurate with respect to how you are moving. But there is a whole other world available to you.

Following are a few of the major myths or false assumptions that inform our experience of what it means to move our bodies. If balance, force, and flow make sense, these myths can't.

1. Movement Myth: One needs to tighten the body in order to move. Yes, muscles do have to engage to move. But you don't have to tighten your entire body to engage these muscles.

2. Movement Myth: One can put oneself in the right position. Yes, there is an optimal configuration. However, you can't *put* yourself in the "right" position, because the optimal configuration is dynamic, constantly moving. All positioning does is interfere with the coordination of the whole.

3. Movement Myth: The body moves in parts. Yes, you do have arms and legs and so on, each of which can be moved independently. However, they are all interconnected. For example, your trapezius muscle is part of your neck, your arm, and your back. In reality you move in *patterns*.

4. Movement Myth: Excess force equals control. Excess force will make you feel as if you have control, but it will cause compression and limit joint movement. Although it can make you feel as if you will succeed, it will actually block physical expression.

All of these assumptions limit movement and exclude balance, force, and flow. This means that they are myths that don't help you move. They are rooted in a fear of failure and a desire to do a good job.

1. All of the myths stop movement. They block joints. When oppositional movement is blocked, excess force is necessary and movement cannot flow through the whole body. Movement myths are static. Consequently, all of the myths block your capacity for expression.
2. All of the myths about movement create a lag time between your intention and the movement you want to make. They take you out of the moment.
3. All the preceding movement myths are just variations on the myth that *extra work equals control and success.*

Now, can you say to yourself that you believe that these movement myths (ideas, concepts, generalizations, or assumptions) no longer make any sense and never could?

YOUR FRAME OF REFERENCE

Make sure you are truly convinced that the myths are really false assumptions so that you will be able to give them up. If not, you will be trying to fit your new experiences into your old frame of reference. Students will sometimes say to me, "But this doesn't feel right." I tell them that they are comparing this new experience to how it felt habitually.

How something feels habitually is familiar, and we equate familiarity with being right. However, how your movement felt habitually probably is out of balance, requiring too much effort and limiting flow.

It is important for understanding and experiencing the awareness exercises in this book that you do not filter these experiences through your old ideas, concepts, past experiences, and assumptions.

Recap: Balance, Force, Flow, Mind

The components of motion are balance, force, and flow, plus your mind.

Static balance (imbalance) inhibits the flow of movement through the body and requires excess force. Dynamic balance allows the entire body to work together, to flow with an economy of force.

You can use the three physical dynamics (balance, force, and flow) as a context for analyzing and understanding your own movement patterns and habits.

With your new awareness, you will evaluate movement through balance, force, and flow instead of through habits and familiarity. Your index for observation becomes, "Am I more balanced? Does it take less effort? Is more of me moving?"

Before any meaningful change can occur, you must first add the nonphysical dynamic: your mind. If you want to improve the efficiency of your movement, you will need to gain an awareness of what you are doing.

My advice is: Don't be in a hurry to be correct. Give yourself time to become familiar with what you think you are doing. Then *overdo* it. Overemphasize your habit so you can really experience what you're doing. This will make you aware of the ways you habitually move (i.e., of muscles that you habitually tighten in order to move).

The general rule for what we are learning is that *everything is moving*. So ask yourself, "Is the surface of my body soft (not taut)? Is everything moving? Does what I am doing allow movement? Does it stop movement?"

Stopping movement will not contribute to artistic expression.

Think of the tai chi symbol. There is a tiny dot of black in the white and a tiny dot of white in the black. The point of the dots is that nothing is as simple as black and white. You can't say, "Never do this." There is always a tiny dot of possibility. So like everything else, even our general rule must include dynamic stillness as well as movement.

When you know what you are doing, it's much easier to choose if you want to continue doing it or not. The goal is to increase your awareness. If you are in a hurry for a quick fix, it will be much harder to effect long-term change. So be patient.

Freedom of movement allows expression.

Part Two

Dynamic Movement

The whole of science is nothing more than a refinement of everyday thinking.

—ALBERT EINSTEIN

Chapter 3

Alignment/Centering and Support

In the book *Sports Speed*, George Dintiman, Bob Ward, and Tom Tellez offered an invaluable observation: "Often athletes feel that they have to 'bear down' and 'stay low and pull' in order to run fast. The scientific analysis of running suggests just the opposite. Reaching maximum speed depends greatly upon how relaxed you can keep your body in a naturally upright position."

This is also true outside sports. The goal is to be relaxed and naturally upright while you are involved in any activity.

What Is Alignment?

Ida P. Rolf pointed out in *Rolfing* that "all schools of body mechanics agree that good posture calls for a vertical alignment of five significant body landmarks—the midpoint of the ear, shoulder joint, hip joint, knee, and ankle" and that "a body so constructed is in static alignment."

When you visit your doctor's office, you sometimes see a chart of the skeletal system on the wall. It's easy to assume that this chart illustrates the correct standing position.

After all, people always seem to be telling you to sit up or stand up straight, or else they say, "This is how to align and hold yourself." It is no wonder most of us start off assuming that alignment is simply a matter of putting our body parts into the proper arrangement and keeping ourselves there.

But there is one important difference between the doctor's chart and you. *You are moving, and the chart isn't.*

So what is alignment? Alignment is a dynamic state of balance that allows your joints to be available to shifts in weight.

The Line of Balance

What the medical chart shows us is the optimal configuration of the skeletal system—the proper interrelationship of the bones and joints for optimal balance and distribution of weight in an upright position.

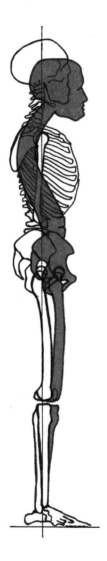

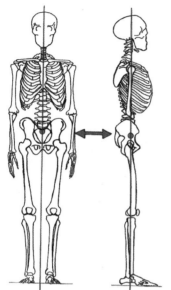

The last chapter discussed the line of balance and the human skeleton. A later chapter provides examples of how your weight distribution in relation to the body's center of gravity (the spot where the body's weight is centered) affects your ease of movement. This illustration shows the body's center of gravity and the line of balance through the body.

As noted in chapter 2, the line of balance, also called the "fall line of gravity," passes through the ankle, the knee, the hip joint, the body's center of gravity (in the pelvis, just above the hip joint), the shoulder, and the atlanto-occipital joint (where your head attaches on top of your spine) just below the ears.

From the front view, it passes between the legs.

Your support is organized around this line of balance. This idea is a huge thought shift for many people, because most think that their support comes from their back.

Three-Dimensional vs. Two-Dimensional

Most people think of themselves in two dimensions—front and back. If I asked you to draw a picture of yourself, you would probably draw only a front view of your body.

This static two-dimensional concept (front and back) inhibits the opposition of movement necessary for counterbalance. Any movement without the counterbalancing motion will cause a compensation (adjustment to imbalance) that uses excess muscular force and interrupts flow.

When I ask people, "Where is your spine?" they put their hands on their backs. When I ask them where their heads attach, they put their hands on the backs of their heads. They assume the back is the place where their support is. Again, they are thinking two-dimensionally.

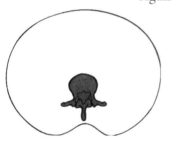

In point of fact, your spine is much more central. The front of your lumbar (lower back) spinal column is exactly dead center in the torso. The spine itself occupies the back half of the torso. This will be explained more specifically later, in the anatomy section of this volume (part 3).

This cross section shows one of the spine's lumbar vertebrae within the human body as viewed from above (with the front of the body at the top of the illustration).

Movement Happens around the Spine

Movement happens around the spine, not in front of your back. Remember the illustrations of looking to the right in chapter 1: the female model first moved two-dimensionally when she looked to the right, moving only her head; then she allowed the entire body to move around the spine, including the back in her movement. Once you give up the front/back two-dimensional model of support, you can experience movement happening around your spine (i.e., moving the weight and volume of the body) three-dimensionally.

As you give up the idea of your support coming from the back, you will be able to reduce excess force and improve the quality of your movement (flow and balance). It takes more effort to hold things still than to let them move. So more effort is required when you limit yourself to a two-dimensional movement pattern, because you must hold yourself still, restricting both movement and expression.

I tell my acting students that when they think of themselves in two dimensions, it's as if they are living their lives on a proscenium stage. But life happens in the round.

Like a Revolving Door

Most people move like the hinged door to their room. They will tighten one side and move only the other. A person turning to the left commonly will hold the left side still. The left side will "hold its breath," and the turn will happen primarily on the right side of the body.

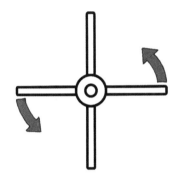

We want to move with opposition, like a revolving door in a hotel lobby. As you turn to the left, your left hip goes back while your right hip comes forward.

Moving the Line of Support

What we want to do is change our concept of support from our back (as shown on the left in the following drawing) to where it really is, more centrally located (as shown on the right in the drawing).

A relaxed body will align itself easily and naturally in gravity, so that body mass balances lightly on the skeleton with a minimum of muscular effort . . . Muscles are not meant to support weight directly, but align the skeleton to support the body in gravity.

—RALPH STRAUCH, *The Feldenkrais Method and Posture*

Your Organs Help with Support

As with movement, your body's support is three-dimensional. The volume of your torso and organs helps support the body.

If you were to fill a plastic shopping bag with water balloons, the bag would have weight, mass, and a degree of self-support. This is what you have resting on your pelvic bowl.

Between your diaphragm and your pelvic bowl, you have this "bag" filled with "water balloons"—your internal organs. It's called the *abdominal cavity*.

If you took a round water balloon and started wrapping a piece of string around the entire balloon, you could eventually change the shape of it to make it more elongated. The surface tension created by the string wrapping would allow the new shape to stand vertically; it would support itself.

If you think of the entire abdominal cavity as one large water balloon, you can see that the muscles of your torso aid in your support in the same way—by wrapping around the entire abdominal cavity.

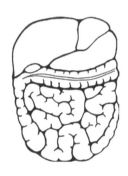

When you move, you are moving the abdominal cavity, including its volume and weight. When you are standing, you are balancing this volume and weight.

Standing Is Dynamic

Standing is a dynamic interplay between weight and energy. Think of your pelvis and abdominal cavity as the central weight and of your head as the counterweight. These two weights are connected by a flexible column—your spine.

When you are standing upright, the weight of your head is balancing over the volume and weight of the abdominal cavity, which rests in the pelvic bowl at the base of the torso. Your head and torso are supported by two columns (the legs). The columns of the upper legs balance over the columns of the lower legs. These columns and your whole body are balanced over your ankles and the tripod of the feet.

String Metaphor

The body is like a string.

Alignment is like straightening the string. If you pull on both ends of a string, the string straightens. There is no need to worry where the curves go. Everything simply falls into alignment. Or in the body's case, everything "falls into" support and balance if you allow your natural suspension.

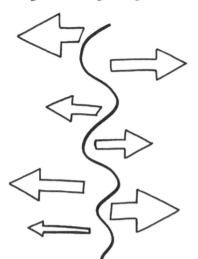

TWO SKELETONS

The shaded area in the first view of the skeletons shown here illustrates the compensatory pattern most people exhibit. Notice how much of this shaded area is in front of the line of balance.

The second view shows the skeleton balanced around the centerline.

Look at the head of the balanced skeleton, and notice how much of the head is behind the centerline. Look at the foot, and notice that the heel is behind the centerline as well.

As illustrated in the second view, the back of the head goes up, the heel goes down, and your "string" straightens (i.e., the curves elongate as the body comes into balance).

Allowing the Body to Align Itself

In class, I use the following movement study: I have my students lie on the floor, and I push on their toes. This is to simulate the pattern of compression that occurs when they put their weight on the front part of the feet while standing.

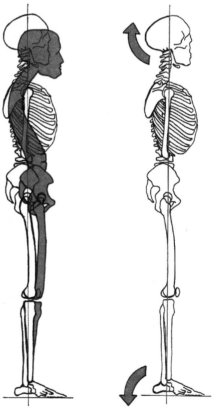

As I push, the students observe how the body compresses as shown in the next illustration. Notice how the head and neck go into compression and how the neck curve is exaggerated.

I then place my hands on the students' heels and pull. As I pull, the compression in the head and neck disappears. You can see that the curve of the neck has disappeared in the next illustration.

This exercise is used to illustrate how the "position" of the head can be changed without focusing on the relationship between the head, neck, and chest. The point is that aligning the body is not a matter of "fixing" a *part* that it is out of place but a process of allowing the body patterns to work together efficiently to reach dynamic alignment. The parts take care of themselves—like the string.

Body alignment can be compared to what happens when you are sailing in a boat that is heeling over. If the boat starts to go over too far, you don't need to stop, get out of the boat, and get everything straightened up again. If you just let go of the line holding the mainsail, the boat will right itself. In the same way, if you stop holding and let go of the tension in your various joints and muscles, allowing movement, your body is designed to "right" itself and come into alignment.

Standing Still Is an Illusion

Standing is the act of balancing the weight of your entire body in relation to the line of balance. The act of standing still is a dynamic process in which you are actually balancing between falling and righting yourself.

I have a childhood memory of a black-and-white film of soldiers standing at attention. As the film was sped up, I could see the soldiers start bobbing forward and back.

A friend who is an osteopath tells me that when you are standing "still" (assuming everything is following nature's design), your calf muscles are constantly working, adjusting to the subtle changes in weight required to maintain balance.

It's all a balancing act. If something goes forward, something must go back. If something goes right, something must go left. If you rotate, there is a counterrotation. It all happens around the line of balance and around your center of gravity.

If you are balancing dynamically, your joints are free to flow with the shifts of weight. Your job is to let this dynamic relationship happen.

Redefining Alignment

A new definition of alignment must be dynamic, not static. According to our new definition, the joints are balanced and available for movement. Dynamic alignment is applicable when you are moving (running, jumping, sitting, squatting), no matter what physical configuration you might find yourself in at any given time. Dynamic alignment is also applicable when you are simply standing.

Alignment as a Constantly Moving Process

Alignment must include allowing the entire body to be available to move as one (flow), constantly balancing and counterbalancing (balance), with an economy of muscular energy (force).

Simply put, alignment is not about how you look, it's about how available you are to move. So the problem is not where the parts are but *what's not moving*. When I coach performers and athletes, I look for what's not moving. If it doesn't move, it's not in concert with the natural design for motion of the body.

Remember this picture of a baby from the overture? I assure you, the last thing in the world a baby is thinking about is aligning itself. It just happens, for free. Your body wants to be in balance. Your body will naturally align itself if you let it.

Chapter 4

Motion and Compensation

The more dramatically powerful a scene is, the greater the call on your inner forces, the freer your body must be.

—CONSTANTIN STANISLAVSKI, IN STANISLAVSKI
AND PAVEL RUMYANTSEV, *Stanislavski on Opera*

Dynamic movement incorporates balance, force, and flow. When our movements are not dynamically balanced, we rely on compensations to keep us in a state of static imbalance.

The Pattern of Compensation

We can learn a lot about movement patterns and our compensations for imbalance from studying illustrations of the body in motion.

The figures in the following illustration show a typical movement pattern that demonstrates the compensations we make when our movements are out of balance.

In the first figure shown here, the student is walking, and her first foot is planted.

The second figure shows the student when she has just finished walking, and her second foot has come to rest. (Notice that you can see her lower back).

Although the student has stopped moving her feet by the third figure, her pelvis continues moving forward as the arrow indicates. Notice that the student's weight is forward of the line of balance and that her lower back has "disappeared."

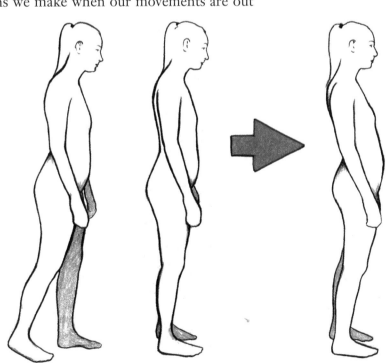

Let's analyze the pattern of compensations the body makes when coming to a stop out of balance. In reality, the process of compensations is not linear; but for clarity, I will explain them in a logical order.

First, in an effort to compensate for the pelvis being forward, the body's weight transfers to the front part of the foot. The overall forward thrust takes weight off the heels and puts more weight on the toes, which grip in an effort to hold you up, causing the feet and ankles to tense. (Some students might also hyperextend their knees. Hyperextension takes place when the knee is pushed too far back—which happens when the knees are locked.) As the legs angle forward, the arch of the lower back must increase. Then the chest collapses and the head juts forward. Finally, the neck compresses to change the angle of the head so you can see where you are going.

Almost every performance student will initially organize his or her standing posture on this model. There are a few variations, but all in all, I see this general pattern in just about everyone (some more than others).

When your pelvis goes forward, out of balance, you become static. You have decreased your ability to move. If your hips are not free to move, you are not as available to express yourself. Consequently, your posture is getting in the way of your performance—whether you are an actor, yoga practitioner, musician, or athlete.

A Series of Compensations

Why must this pattern of compensation happen? If some part of your body goes forward of the line of balance and there is no oppositional movement, there must be a compensation to balance the weight that is now out of balance. That compensation equals compression and excess force, which, in turn, limit movement.

In the situation we've been discussing (walking and then coming to a stop out of balance), your pelvis goes forward after you stop walking. If your lower back didn't compensate, you'd be standing like the person on the left in the next illustration. (Actually, you wouldn't be standing at all, because you'd fall over unless you were able to stop in front of some sort of support like the chair shown in the illustration.)

For you to stand with your pelvis forward of the line of balance, your legs must angle forward from the ankles to the pelvis.

To compensate for the forward thrust of the pelvis, your feet, ankles, knees, and hips must tighten.

Because your pelvis is so far forward, you must compensate by increasing the curvature of your lower back (lumbar spine) to keep from falling over, as shown in the center illustration.

Since it is not advantageous or attractive to walk around looking at the ceiling, you must compensate by pulling down on your chest (upper spine or thorax), head, and neck, as shown in the illustration on the right. Each compensation leads to another.

Attachment of the Head to the Spine

Your head attaches to the top of your spine, just below the ears.

However, when your body is in the pattern of compensation previously discussed, you tend to move your head as if the head joint were lower in the neck, by the shoulders.

As noted in the discussion of someone standing with the pelvis thrust forward, a series of compensations takes place.

Because of the lower back compensation in relation to the pelvis being thrust forward, you compress the chest in order to get your head forward, closer to balance. Then you compress your neck so that you can see where you are going; in doing so, you move your

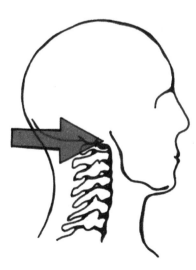

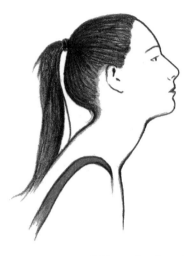

head as if the joint that connects it to the neck were lower than it really is.

In the illustration at left, you can see this awkward positioning with the kind of slump that is especially observable when a person sits and collapses.

Awareness of the Compensation

You can see how the whole pattern of compensation is a simple case of cause and effect. When the pelvis goes forward, the spine must compensate. When the head goes back, the spine must compensate. All these compensations cause compression and limit movement.

Once you understand the cause for the pattern of compensation, it makes the whole process much easier to sort out. It is impossible to "fix" one part that is out of balance if you don't consider how all the compensations affect each other. This is why positioning yourself cannot work: you are not considering the whole pattern.

The problem, then, is one of awareness. Your habit of compensation has become so ingrained that you don't know you are doing it. The challenge is how to make yourself aware of what you are doing (i.e., of what has become habitual for you).

Reverse Compensatory Pattern

Because their focus is toward the audience, most performers balance forward, with their weight on their toes, as in our previous examples. However, there are other performers who do the reverse: they put most of their weight on their heels, as shown in the drawing here on the right.

The body's weight is designed to be distributed over the whole foot. When that weight is put on the heels, the compensations will be somewhat different from what we've been describing.

But with either compensatory pattern (weight on toes or weight on heels), we are still dealing with imbalance and the compensations for imbalance. Once an individual becomes aware of his or her pattern, including its cause and effect, it becomes easier to make a change.

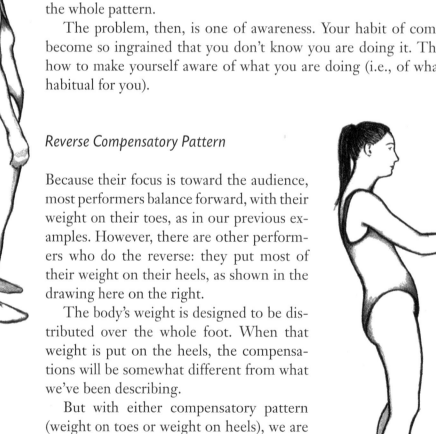

The Baby Study: The Formula for Movement

Our goal is to move without the compensations we've been discussing. The ease of movement we hope to achieve can be seen by observing a baby making a simple movement, such as rolling over.

This baby has the intention to roll over. Rather than tightening in order to move, her joints are available for movement.

The baby uses her weight to her advantage. She follows the weight of her legs and arms as she rolls.

The baby retains her suspension, and her body expands from head to foot.

The baby has achieved her objective and is ready for her next intention.
Throughout this series, the baby has moved with balance, force, and flow. How would you roll over?

Light at the End of the Tunnel

Most people can appreciate that there is no need to continue compensating once you eliminate the cause of the compensation.

All at once, the habitual extra effort (force) involved in maintaining the imbalance becomes obvious to you, and you realize you don't need to compensate any more. You can allow movement. It's your choice: you're in charge.

The Drawer Metaphor

Change doesn't happen all at once. Consider this example from everyday life. In our kitchen is a four-drawer cabinet. When our children were little, we put our flatware in the second drawer from the top. This way, the little guys could reach their own spoons and help set the table.

After my son graduated from high school and headed off to college, it occurred to us that we could move our flatware back to the top drawer. Do you have any idea how many times I have gone to the second drawer for a spoon?

Little by little, I seem to be going to the top drawer more often now. If I am distracted, if someone is talking to me, I may go to the second drawer. But if I am going for a spoon and am not distracted, I'll go for the top drawer. After some number of days or weeks, I will no longer go to the second drawer.

A performer undergoes pretty much the same process when you start to change your movement patterns. Perhaps it's even a little harder for the performer, because you may not even realize you are going to the second drawer. The only means at your disposal that will help you be aware of what you're doing is to notice when you are moving in a habitual manner. Think about that: you have to notice your habits. That's tough, because habits, by virtue of being habits, are unconscious.

Also, when you move habitually, you are still able to perform—just not with as much expression. For the performer, this is like having spoons in both drawers. (I wonder how long it would take me to change if I had spoons in both drawers.) So be gentle with yourself. You will get there. It is a matter of time and intention.

Chapter 5
Moving with Suspension

A person may reveal nothing of himself and then, suddenly, make a movement that contains a whole autobiography.
—GEORGE SEGAL

The body is designed to retain suspension and be available for motion, as your joints become available to shifts in weight and as you follow your intention. With every breath and every movement, your spine is contracting and expanding.

A Definition of Suspension

I picked up the term *suspension* from dressage riders (who give barely perceptible signals to their horses to enable them to execute precision movement patterns). As I understand it, *suspension* describes how a horse retains its volume when it is moving well. That's what is meant to happen to us, too. Our bodies have a certain dynamic volume (we are constantly breathing), and we retain that volume when we move.

Most of us compress our bodies and lose suspension in order to move. When you lose suspension, everything requires more effort. Your body has a certain length that is flexible (a capacity for expanding and contracting). There is no need to compress the body (slump) and no need to stretch it (stand up straight). As with a spring, you simply let the body occupy the volume it occupies.

Sponge Metaphor

A metaphor that explains suspension involves a sponge. When you put a dry sponge in water, the whole thing expands: it has suspension. The suspension happens in all directions as the sponge fills out. It's the same with your body. Suspension doesn't happen in just one direction—up (the direction that we think of as perfect posture). It is a whole-body thing, happening in all directions (up and down, front to back, and side to side).

Suspension is maintaining the body's volume while moving.

Muscles and Suspension

Muscles maintain volume (suspension) as they support and stabilize. This is an important idea, because it provides you with a reason why *you don't have to tighten joints to hold yourself.*

Obviously, muscles have to engage in order for you to breathe, to maintain balance, and to move. What I am referring to when I talk about tightening is excess muscular effort that causes compression in the joints and restricts movement.

When you tighten muscles unnecessarily, not only do you limit your suspension and disrupt your body's ability to counterbalance, but you also make yourself weaker, because the muscles shorten and don't have as much length to contract. You then must overwork to get the same results, making everything you do more difficult and less efficient. Up to a certain point, the longer the muscle is, the stronger it is. (Physiologically, there is an optimum muscle length; but for our purposes, the point is that tensing/shortening makes you weaker, not stronger.)

Compression Is Easy to Demonstrate

The following exercise demonstrates the way we compress our bodies during a simple movement: standing up from a seated position.

AWARENESS STUDY: Moving from Sitting in a Chair to Standing

1. First, sit back and relax. Now stand up.

The first thing you'll probably notice is that you tightened and compressed your body in order to stand. Perhaps you also held your breath or tightened your stomach. If you didn't notice this habit, try standing up faster.

What if that extra tightening were completely unnecessary? It is! Why would you have to hold your breath to stand up? That thought is just an implied limitation. All you achieve by tightening and compressing is that you ruin your suspension and keep yourself from being in balance. The key is to allow movement.

2. Try standing again *without tightening.*

At this point, it probably seems impossible to stand up without first tightening. I realize muscles have to engage for you to stand. But see if you can stand up with a just little less overall tightening.

See, you could do it. Now think about that. Over the course of your life, that approach adds up to a lot of energy conservation.

Remember, these movement changes don't have to happen all at once. The point of these studies is not to be "right." There's no need to be perfect. Just notice what happens; don't judge yourself.

What you are gaining is increased awareness. If you never thought about how your body tightens, becoming somewhat rigid or taut, when you stand, you would use that much extra effort every time you stand up for the rest of your life. So in the long run, even this first small change (moving with a little less tightening) is a significant step toward real progress.

The compression that you create in order to stand doesn't automatically go away after you stand either. Through habit, you continue to maintain this pattern of compression, and it affects every movement that you make after you stand. When you compress your body, you lose suspension, you don't allow your spine to expand, and all your movements take more effort.

Efficient movement begins with *allowing* rather than tightening.

Allowing Expansion

When, upon noticing that you are holding your body unnecessarily tense (which you do when you compress in order to move), you release that tension, you don't get all soft and floppy. The reason for this is that although floppy is the opposite of taut, the opposite of compression is expansion. Therefore, the release of tension allows movement, and the volume of your body expands into a state of balanced dynamic suspension. You remain vital!

When you let go of everything, you can easily collapse (become floppy). But you don't need to throw the main circuit breaker. When you get floppy, you are throwing away your intention with your tension. Instead, allow the expansion to occur as you release the tension.

The Formula for Movement

According to the new formula for movement that I recommend for you, *you have the intention to move, and simultaneously the joints are available to accommodate the shifts in weight as you move.*

The efficiency of your movement (balance, force, and flow) is determined by how available you are to the weight shifts and to what degree you use your weight to your advantage as you move. Movement means moving weight and volume (suspension).

How Weight and Intention Initiate Movement

To understand how weight and intention initiate movement, first think of your body differently (outside the box). Using your new formula for movement, think of moving volume (suspension) and weight.

As you begin to move, you may notice tightening that seems to take place on the surface of your body, almost as if you expect your support and your movement to originate from the taut surface of your body. When you conceptualize yourself in three dimensions, with volume and weight, it's easier to get rid of this surface tightening.

However, paying attention to what is happening on the surface is a great tool to gain awareness of your unconscious movement habits. If you feel the surface of your body becoming taut, you know you are not moving efficiently.

The second thought shift is for you to consider using the weight of your body to your advantage. Think of yourself as one of those inflatable punching toys with sand in the bottom. It falls over when punched and then rights itself. The reason a punching toy can right itself is that its weight is in the bottom. As the weight goes down, the toy goes up. This is the key: the punching toy *follows the weight*.

Rather than using force to move back from a knocked-over position to an upright position, the punching toy rights itself because the weight responds to gravity and goes down. As the weight goes down, the back-to-vertical movement just happens. That's the key to how we move.

The subsequent weight shift of your body in relation to your intention initiates movement as the joints become available. To be available means that your joints are unencumbered by tension and free to accommodate changes in the weight distribution of your body. You will then move from suspension rather than compression.

Therefore, your new movement formula is (and remember that these "steps" happen simultaneously), "I have the intention to move. My joints become (or are) available. I follow the weight."

To explore the idea of how people move, let's look at a couple of simple studies of how you might move from sitting in a chair and leaning forward to sitting upright.

AWARENESS STUDY: Moving Front-to-Back the Old Way

The old movement formula you've been using would have been, "I have the intention to move; I tighten up; I move." Let's see how this old way of working influences your movement.

1. Sit on the front edge of a standard wooden chair or the equivalent.
2. Start in a position of leaning forward, as shown on the left in the illustration that follows.
3. Move to an upright sitting position, as shown on the right in the illustration.
4. Lean forward and then move to an upright position a couple of times.

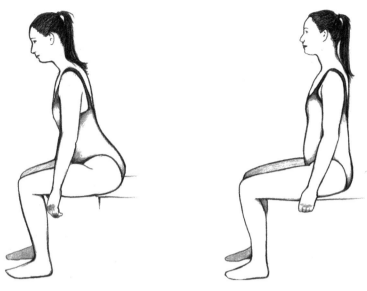

You may or may not have noticed that you overengaged your muscles to move forward and then tightened to move back again. The reason you needed to tighten before moving is that you were not using your weight to your advantage. You were actually working against yourself.

One of the causes of this inefficient way of moving is the way in which you conceptualized the movement.

I think it is safe to say that most people would conceive of this movement (from leaning forward to sitting upright) as moving from front-to-back, as indicated by the arrow in this illustration.

AWARENESS STUDY: Following the Weight

Now we are going to explore a new option: following the weight.

1. As before, start in a sitting position, leaning forward slightly, as shown in the illustration to the left.

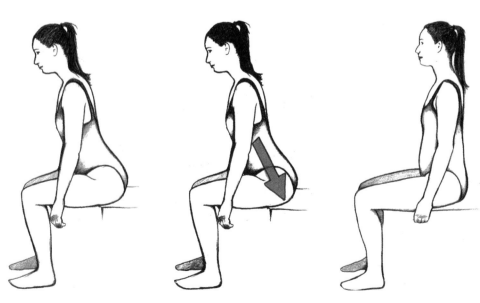

2. Then allow your hips to be available (to the weight shift), and let your weight move downward toward the chair.

As with the punching toy, following the weight will make it easier for you to move back to vertical, as shown in this illustration. The movement backward is a by-product of allowing your weight to go down. When you are able to sort it out, you will be amazed at how little effort this new way of moving requires.

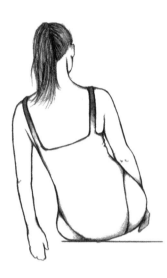

The results of following the weight may be even more obvious when you look at what happens when you lean to the side and then move back to vertical.

Notice in this illustration that when leaning to the left, the individual's right hip is in the air. It seems absurd to tighten up the hips in order to *pull* that raised hip back down to the chair.

As shown below, all you have to do to return to vertical is to allow your left hip joint to move. Then let gravity help you. If you follow your weight, your right hip will go back down to the chair with no extra effort.

You have just made a huge change in how you initiate and conceptualize movement. Rather than becoming taut or rigid in order to move, you have just moved in the exact opposite way. You have initiated movement by *allowing* rather than tightening. This is a huge change in the overall efficiency of your movement. It is also a major change in your potential for physical expression. Instead of closing yourself down, you are opening up. Instead of excluding, you are including.

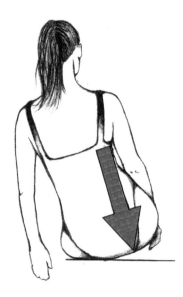

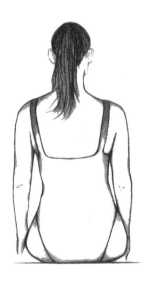

A large portion of your weight is in your abdominal cavity. The weight of your body wants to follow gravity and go down. But initially in the example of leaning forward and returning to upright, you weren't using this weight to your advantage, because you were only thinking of moving in one direction: *back*.

In this process, you were tightening the surface of your body and your joints to move in that one direction.

Now, instead of thinking of the movement as being from front to back, you can conceptualize the movement as following your weight *down*, as demonstrated with the punching toy and the awareness study "Following the Weight."

When the hip joints aren't locked, the movement originates from a very different place and happens in a very different way. Instead of taking place at the waistline, the movement happens lower, nearer to the surface of the chair. More of you is now available to move with your intention. This is a good example of how you can include more of yourself when you move, so that you become more expressive.

Suspension and the Volume of the Torso

As I've noted, when most people think of sitting up straight, they are actually thinking that they have to push themselves up from the back.

But if you pay attention as you push through your back to sit upright, you'll notice that you aren't pushing only through your back.

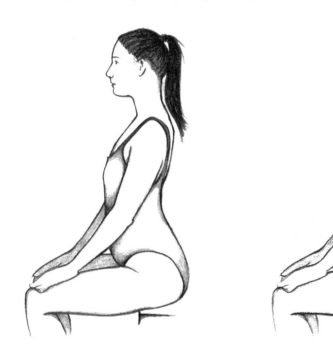

In order to push "up" from your back, you must have someplace to push from. So you tighten your hips and most likely your knees and feet as well. If your hips are tight, you can't use your weight to your advantage.

When you sit and push through your back to stay upright, your torso adopts the kidney bean shape in the illustration below.

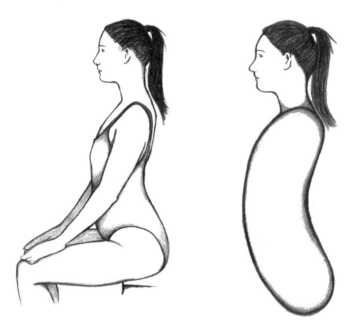

When you slump, you still have the kidney bean shape. It is just in the opposite direction, as shown in the following illustration.

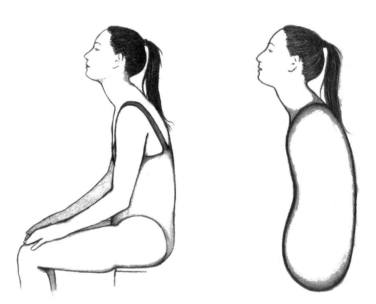

As you can see, when you slump, your breastbone (sternum) and upper torso move forward, with an accompanying compression of the abdominal muscles (i.e., the whole front of the kidney bean compresses). You lose suspension.

You've no doubt guessed it. The direction of the kidney bean doesn't matter: either direction is out of balance and forces you to lock joints.

It has been my experience that when trying to sit up straight by pushing through the back, most of my students push from a spot somewhere around or just above the belt line or waist (the "push spot"), as shown here.

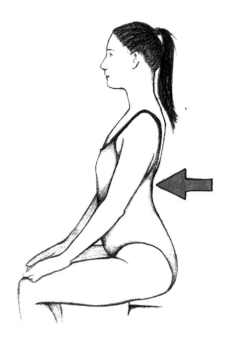

Earlier, I pointed out that when I touch someone with one finger, the person tends to freeze all the surrounding muscles to get a better focus on the spot I'm touching. In the same way, when you move from the "push spot" in your back, you are focusing on just one area. In order to have this spot in your back to push from, you lock up everything around the "push spot" when you push to sit up straight. When you slump, essentially what you are doing is relaxing this "push spot" and collapsing.

These movements are complementary opposites: you go out of balance in one direction (the "push" kidney bean), and then you go out of balance in the other direction (the "slump" kidney bean). The problem is that you can go back and forth like this forever because both directions are out of balance.

The Balanced Bean

For balanced posture, we want to be somewhere in the middle of the two kidney beans: we want to be in more of a balanced bean shape, as shown in this illustration.

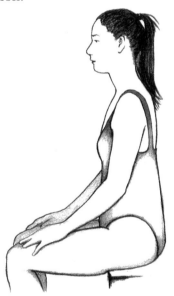

I do not mean to suggest that the spine is perfectly straight. It actually has very distinctive curves, which I'll discuss in a later chapter. The idea of the balanced bean shape is simply a metaphor to help you find balance between the two kidney bean extremes.

One reason the balanced bean option is so difficult for you to find is that, most likely, you are using the push spot near your waist as your frame of reference.

Consequently, you are not getting your awareness low enough to make a change. Think of sitting as being organized from the chair and not from your lower back. Let the weight of your abdominal cavity and torso go all the way to the chair.

The real direction of sitting is down *and* up. Your thinking has to be balanced. The weight must be allowed to go all the way to the chair, while the spine and torso are expanding and contracting with your breath and movement.

Finding Dynamic Suspension

If you want to move the way you were designed to move and increase your capacity for expression, the weight of your head needs to be supported by the weight and volume of your torso. Your torso needs to be balanced over your sit bones (the bones you sit on—the ones at the base of your pelvic bowl), with the help of your hips being open and available to accommodate movement.

The kidney bean postures interfere with the efficiency of the expansion and contraction of the spine as you breathe and move.

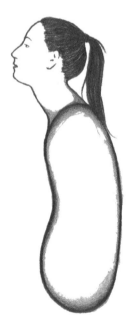 

In these illustrations of both kidney bean postures (slumping and pushing up from the back), you may notice that the compression in the chest doesn't necessarily change.

The head and neck are compressed both ways, either collapsed and compressed or pushed and compressed.

For you to find balance, it is necessary for the weight of your head to be supported by your torso. For that to happen, the pattern of compensation in the upper chest (caused by the head being forward) must change as well.

This is the point at which most people get frustrated. They know the head is not supposed to be thrust forward, so they try to move it back. But moving the head alone won't achieve balance, because the upper chest compensation is still there.

When you try to push or pull your head to where you think it's supposed to be, you are actually making matters worse. Not only do you have the tension of the compensation, but you also have the tension of the attempted correction.

You are attempting to fix a *part* instead of relating the problem of the imbalance to the whole body. You are also trying to make it *look* right instead of focusing on it *moving* right.

To find balance in your torso, head, and neck, you need to remove all of the compensations; that is, all of the parts doing the compensating must be able to move.

Play around with this idea. As you erase the compensations of the kidney beans and become a balanced bean, you'll notice that your sense of weight seems to drop—as we discovered with the punching toy. The weight of your head is now supported over your torso, and the weight of the torso is resting on the chair.

With your body in this configuration, you'll find that moving becomes easier and more efficient. You are now organizing your movement around your spine and around the weight and volume of your torso. You are no longer looking to the surface of your back for your support. You are in dynamic suspension.

Your Head as Counterweight

As you've already learned, most of your weight is located in your hips and abdominal cavity. On the other end of your spine is your head, which functions as a counterweight. If you didn't have the weight of your head to counterbalance the weight of the abdominal cavity, it would be much harder to get out of a chair, because it would take more muscular force.

How the Counterweight Works

The process of standing up organizes over the ankle joint. But most people file their flight plan too early. They try to lift themselves out of the chair too soon.

Notice how it feels when you try to stand from a sitting position while your weight is behind your ankle (as in the illustration to the right), and compare that to how it feels to stand while your weight is over (or in front of) your ankles.

If, as shown in this illustration, you can get enough weight (your head plus your upper torso and shoulder area) in front of your ankles so that you are in balance before liftoff, you will be able to get out of a chair in a much easier way.

The head doesn't need to weigh as much as your abdominal cavity to function as a counterweight, because the weight of your head is on the end of a lever (the spinal column). This lever creates a certain mechanical advantage that is enough to help you counterbalance the weight of the abdominal cavity.

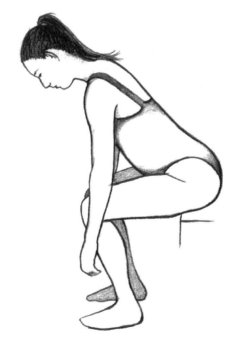

The act of getting up from the chair using the counterweight of the head requires much less effort than you ever dreamed.

The following puzzler aired on the National Public Radio program *Car Talk*. This is how I remember it.

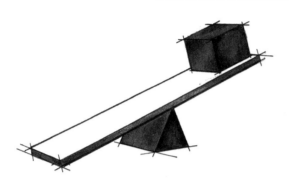

There is a seesaw. The board of the seesaw is one foot wide and eight feet long. It weighs thirty-six pounds. The fulcrum is two feet from one end of the board. Six feet of board are on the other side of the fulcrum. On the short side, there's a solid one-foot-square concrete cube placed right at the end of the board. The cube weighs forty-eight pounds.

How much weight has to be placed on the other end to balance the seesaw?

Puzzler Solved   The answer is zero pounds. Nothing needs to be placed on the other end of the seesaw. It is balanced just the way it is.

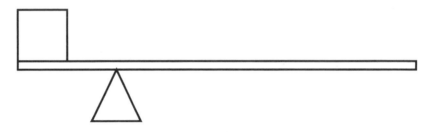

The long side of the board weighs enough to balance the concrete block and two-foot board on the short side. This has to do with the center of mass on the long side being so much farther away from the fulcrum than the center of mass on the short side.

This is a fun way to demonstrate the principle of using a smaller weight (e.g., the head) at the end of a seesaw (e.g., the spine) to balance a greater weight (e.g., the abdominal cavity).

Although this example is helpful, it is imperfect. You have to remember that your "seesaw" (i.e., your spine) is alive and flexible and moves as you breathe.

Putting the Counterweight to Good Use

Now that we've seen how a counterweight functions, let's consider how we can put this knowledge to good use when making a simple movement, such as getting out of a chair.

First, let's consider what happens if we are slumping. Slumping is detrimental to movement for two reasons: not only does slumping impair your spine's ability to lengthen and contract, but it also shortens the "seesaw" (the distance between your sit bones and the top of your head).

This shortening of the torso makes it much more difficult to get enough weight forward of the ankle joint to counterbalance the weight of the abdominal cavity as you stand from sitting. You can see this for yourself by trying the following exercise.

AWARENESS STUDY: The Head and Shoulders as Counterweights

1. While sitting in a chair, slump and then try to get out of the chair.

See how difficult that is? You have shortened the "seesaw," as shown in this illustration.

2. Now sit upright and then, as shown in the next illustration, lean over to get the weight of your head in front of your ankles.

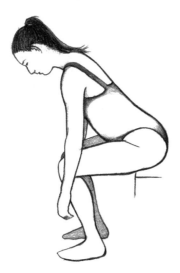

3. Then try to get out of the chair.

By trying it yourself, you can see that using the counterweight of your head effectively makes getting out of the chair much easier.

If you are having trouble sorting out this counterweight function, think about this: you can make your "seesaw" longer and enhance the counterbalancing effect by reaching toward the ceiling with your arms.

Then, as shown in this illustration, you can use the weight of your arms as an additional counterweight to offset the weight of your abdominal cavity.

A LITTLE HINT

If you are still having trouble sorting out the counterweight function for yourself (i.e., if using your head and extended arms as a counterweight still did not make it easier for you to get out of the chair when you tried the previous awareness study), there's a reason it might not be working for you. This movement is affected by other components: your hips and knees.

Think of your head and torso as four stacked balls. The top ball is your head and neck area, the second your chest, the third from your chest to your waist, and the fourth from the waist to the chair.

If you don't allow your hip joints to be part of the movement pattern, you are, in effect, holding the fourth ball (the bottom ball) still. Your movement will then be between the third and fourth balls (at your waist) instead of below the fourth ball (in the hips), where it contacts the chair.

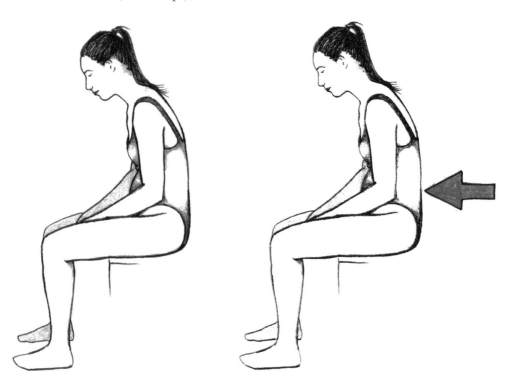

Unless you allow movement in your hip joints, you will find it difficult to get the weight of your head and arms sufficiently forward of your ankles to counterbalance the rest of your body.

 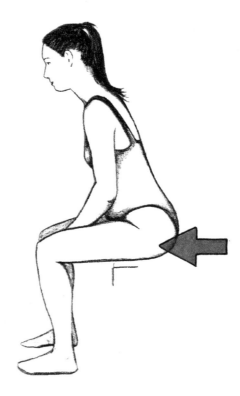

While you try getting up again, see if you can feel the movement happening lower. Feel your sit bones moving.

You may find it helpful to refer to the anatomy section of this book (part 3) for more specific information about the hip joints and sit bones.

The knees are also part of the pattern of counterbalance.

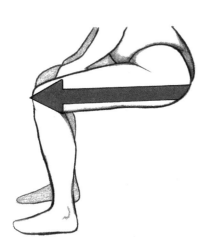

As you start to stand, allow your knees to move forward. The knees must move forward, because they are attached to the femurs, which are attached to the pelvis at the hip joint.

As the pelvis rocks forward, the femurs move forward, and the knees (and, of course, the weight of the knees)

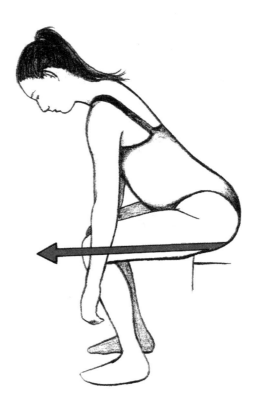

move in front of the ankle joint and help with offsetting the weight of the abdominal cavity while you stand.

It is also helpful to know that your knees bend below the kneecaps. The common idea that your knee bends above the kneecap restricts the forward movement of the knees when you move from sitting to standing. For more on this, see chapter 8.

Allowing the knees (and the weight of the knees) to move forward helps you get your head and torso forward of the body's line of gravity, which passes through your ankle.

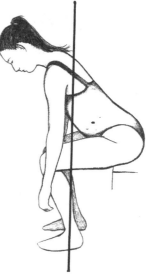

Weight, Movement, Gravity, and Focus

An obvious thing to consider about weight and movement is that weight always goes down, the direction of gravity.

If you let it, gravity will do much of the work to help you move efficiently. Your response to gravity affects the spine's expansion and contraction.

It is easy to grasp how, when you are sitting or standing, gravity's downward pull aids with contraction.

But the concept of expansion of the spine might seem like a contradiction unless you understand that when the spine lengthens, it is actually moving upward and downward at the same time.

The reason you experience only the upward sensation when you allow the spine to expand while you are sitting is that, with the chair directly beneath you, it is not possible for your body to move downward. Therefore, you experience the downward expansion as an upward movement.

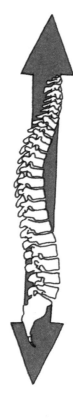

Focus and Suspension

Let's consider what happens to your weight when you want to reach for something above your head. Depending on your focus, you may or may not maintain suspension.

AWARENESS STUDY: Reaching *with* and *without* Expansion

1. While sitting in a chair, reach as high as you can toward the ceiling.

Most likely, when you reach up, you are thinking only about how high you can reach. This single, excluding focus "up" affects how you move.

In order for you to reach "as high as you can," your hips tighten and you push through your back (creating a backward kidney bean). As a result, although you are still in contact with the chair, your weight "leaves the chair"—just like the weight of the person in this illustration.

If you were sitting on a bathroom scale, the scale would register less weight, because some of your weight is being transferred (with a lot of effort) to the legs and feet. (Mimes use this same approach to "sit in a chair" that isn't there.) But it's not necessary for your legs to be working just because you are reaching up.

Even if you are reaching as high as you can while sitting, you don't need to tighten your hips and knees as you make the reaching movement. You may already have made the jump to the next concept: if you let your weight go down as you reach up, there will be less curvature in your back, and you'll actually be able to reach higher.

Your spine can expand in both directions as you reach toward the ceiling. Now the movement flows through the entire body instead of just being in the arm. Instead of the gesture being locked and pushing up, the torso is involved/ included in the reaching movement.

A simple way to apply this idea is to try the next step of this exercise on reaching.

2. Think "down" while you reach up.

See, you can reach higher when you allow expansion of your spine. More of your body is involved. More of your shoulder, arm structure, and spine are available to move.

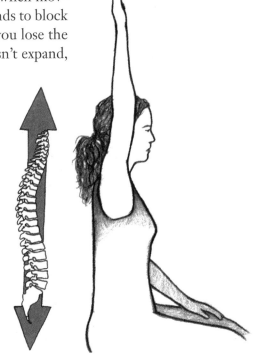

Any time you have a one-directional or singular focus when moving, you are, in effect, not fully available. A single focus tends to block oppositional movement. Your surface becomes taut, and you lose the awareness of moving weight and volume. Your spine doesn't expand, and you lose suspension. That's why students in martial arts training are asked for a soft focus.

As discussed in chapter 2, soft focus means not focusing narrowly on a single point. You take in the surroundings and lose the hardness of the single focus. You allow the softness. Your entire body is available to your intention.

FOCUS FOR STANDING PERFORMANCE

The example of your weight not leaving the chair as you reach and focus "up" also applies to movements made while standing. Your weight does not need to leave the floor.

This concept is especially important for conductors but equally useful to actors, singers, instrumentalists, or anyone who stands up and performs.

One of the first things a conductor does is raise his or her arms. This movement can cause a tension pattern in the entire body. It's as if the conductor's weight leaves the podium as he or she raises the arms.

The concept is the same as reaching up while sitting down. The conductor's body loses suspension as he or she focuses "up."

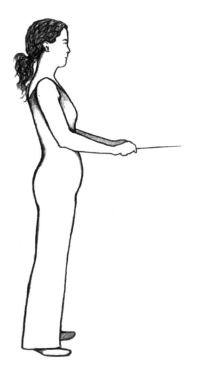

As the conductor with singular focus raises the arms, he or she is also lifting the weight of the upper body. The thought goes up, and the weight goes forward. Then the weight is unequally distributed through the feet, which causes the toes to tense—all of which locks and tightens the body, as shown in this illustration.

This is not a great way to begin is it? In fact, I might go so far as to say that the dynamic balance in your performance is over before you begin. At the least, you have shut down your torso, your spine's ability to expand and contract, and a large percentage of your capacity for expression, just by raising your arms.

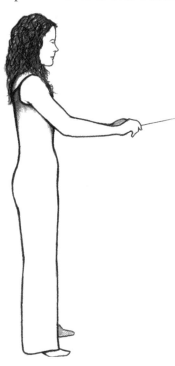

When I suggest to the conductor that the feet can remain soft and that the body's weight doesn't need to leave the floor as his or her arms are raised (even when wearing heels), there is a different distribution of weight and a new quality to his or her movement, as shown in this illustration.

I also suggest that the conductor start to notice how the entire foot remains in contact with the floor.

If the conductor allows it, he or she will begin to feel that the heels as well as the toes are providing support for the body.

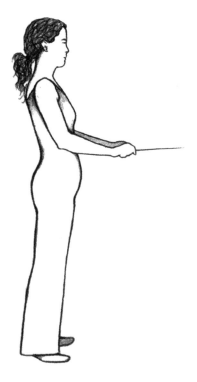

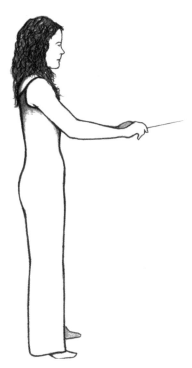

If the whole foot is in contact with the floor and supporting the weight of the body, then the ankle and foot can remain dynamic.

Allowing the weight to remain on the floor enables any standing performer to remain in dynamic balance.

Everything Is Moving

Let's wrap up our ideas about suspension. From the movement studies we've examined so far, we have learned about following our weight, using our weight to our advantage, expanding our focus, and retaining our body's volume while moving.

No matter what gesture or movement we make, everything is moving. It is important to keep this thought in mind in order to keep your entire body available and make movement easier.

Next time you reach toward the ceiling, there are several thoughts that will help you maintain suspension and increase your efficiency and capacity for expression.

1. Focusing *down* is just as important as thinking of reaching *up*. So take in everything, using a soft focus.
2. It is not necessary to tighten. If the surface of your body is taut when you move your arm, you can't use your weight and volume to your advantage.

3. When you move the weight of your arm, the movement flows through the entire body. There is really no such thing as moving only your arm; thinking in parts causes you to tighten.
4. As you raise your arm toward the ceiling, say to yourself, "Everything is moving." Experience your whole body expanding and all the joints being available. You'll notice that the movement is easier.

Alignment and Weight Shift

Alignment is redefined according to your new formula for movement. Rather than the joints of the body being held and positioned, the joints are available to move and, therefore, are balanced.

This definition of alignment will work with every movement that you make. If you follow the weight shift as you move, your joints will be available, and any movement that you make will

1. be aligned or balanced (balance);
2. take place with an economy of effort (force);
3. flow through the entire body, as your spine is expanding and contracting with every movement and every breath (flow).

Losing Suspension

When you gesture with your new formula ("I have the intention to move. My joints are available. I follow the weight"), you will increase your capacity for expression and be more present, because more of your body is now involved in the gesture.

When you tighten to move, you lose suspension, which takes you out of the moment. You are no longer experiencing the gesture.

A DELAYED RESPONSE

When you tighten before you initiate movement (as when you prepare to stand), there is an almost imperceptible pause. This delay separates you from what you are experiencing. It takes you out of the moment. Instead of the movement happening with the intention ("Just do it"), it now becomes work.

When you become taut and rigid, you lose suspension. Then you are unable to resonate with what you are doing—acting, conducting, singing, playing an instrument, playing a sport, or whatever activity you choose.

If you tighten to move instead of allowing the movement to happen in response to your intention, you will not be as expressive, nor will you be as skilled at what you do.

In my classes at the university, I show a video that is a study of a baby moving from sitting to crawling. I show the study backward, so that it looks as if the baby is moving from crawling to sitting.

It is impossible for my students to tell that I'm showing the video backward, because the baby is following her weight and is not betraying her direction of movement with a pattern of tension.

The baby in this picture (taken from the video just mentioned) is not concerned about how she looks. She just moves with her intention and retains her suspension.

As babies, we all did this.

Part Three

The Anatomy of Expression

Not everything that counts can be counted, and not everything that can be counted counts.

—ALBERT EINSTEIN

Chapter 6

A Context for the Body

What a piece of work is a man.
—WILLIAM SHAKESPEARE, *Hamlet*

This look at the body's main structural components, the skeleton and muscles, is intended to give a context for the body and to reveal the potential for movement.

The idea is to substitute specific information about your body for a general understanding that may lead to common assumptions that may or may not be accurate and that most likely limit your capacity for movement.

Bones

When you think of a skeleton, what probably comes to mind is an old rocklike collection of bones wired together in the back of some biology classroom. This dried-up collection of mineral salts is a dead skeleton.

It is important to remember that there is nothing like that inside you. The skeleton inside you is alive; inside the bones, the marrow manufactures blood. As you run and jump, the living bones torque and spring. There is nothing rocklike about a living skeleton. It is dynamic. George B. Bridgman provided another way of thinking about it: "Bones constitute the pressure system of the body. In them are expressed, therefore, laws of architecture, as in the dome of the head, the arches of the foot, the pillars of the legs, etc.; and laws of mechanics, such as the hinges of the elbows, the levers of the limbs, etc." (*Constructive Anatomy*).

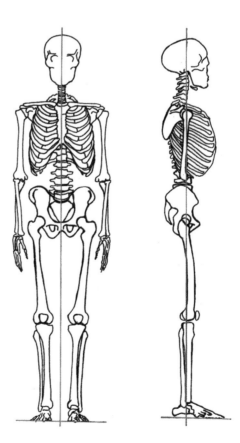

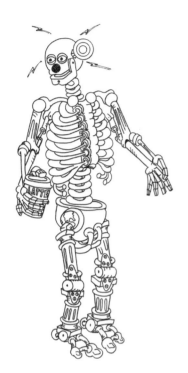

The Dynamic Skeleton

Let's look at the various parts of the skeleton, presented as a collection of everyday shapes, and examine how they connect with each other. Of course, although I discuss individual parts, keep in mind that the body functions as a whole and that everything is moving.

The BASE of the skeleton is a flexible tripod (foot).

A CYLINDER (ankle) is on top of the tripod.

A COLUMN (lower leg) with a concave bottom balances on top of the cylinder.

A HINGE (knee) connects the lower leg column to a FLYING BUTTRESS (upper leg). (A flying buttress is a support in the form of a semiarch, frequently located on the outside of a building, for instance, the Cathedral of Notre Dame in Paris.)

A BALL (hip joint) is at the top of each flying buttress.

Each ball fits into a LITTLE CUP (hip socket).

Each cup is on the side of a LARGE BOWL (pelvic girdle).

The bowl is at the base of a SPRING (spine).

Around the spring are twenty PAIL HANDLES and four HALF HANDLES (ribs).

A flexible MILKMAID'S YOKE (the arm structure) is located at the top of the rib cage.

ROBOT CRANES (arms) hang from each side of the yoke.

A FIVE-PRONGED GRIPPER (hand) is on the end of each crane.

A COUNTERWEIGHT (head) is on top of the spring and thus at the top of the skeleton.

MISCONCEPTIONS AND ASSUMPTIONS

I've worked with all kinds of performing artists, actors, athletes, musicians, college students, conductors, and business professionals. Regardless of a person's background or reason for working with me, people usually have the same misconceptions about how the body is put together.

A list of ideas about the body follows. After each common misconception people have about how the body parts are put together are statements describing where the parts really are.

Following each item in this list is a set of pictures illustrating the difference between the assumption that people make and the reality of human anatomy.

About twenty years ago, Alexander Technique teachers Barbara and Bill Conable introduced me to this method of sorting out assumptions, which they call "body mapping."

As the Conables describe it, a body map is one's self-representation in one's own brain. The individual's understanding of his or her body may create an accurate or inaccurate body map.

The following common misconceptions lead to inefficient movement.

1. Assumption: The head attaches at the back. In reality, the head attaches more centrally, at the atlanto-occipital joint.

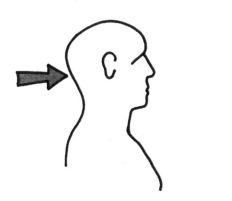
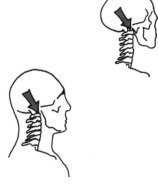

2. Assumption: The arms attach at the shoulders. In reality, the bone-to-bone attachment between your arm and torso is at the sternoclavicular joint.

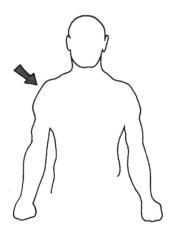
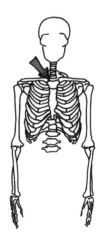

3. Assumption: The ribs are near the vertical center of the torso. In reality, yes, but your ribs are also higher in the chest. Your first rib is higher than your collarbone, toward the rear.

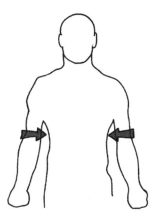
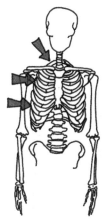

4. Assumption: The middle of the body is where the waist is. In reality, the center of gravity of your body is below your waist (at sacral vertebra 2).

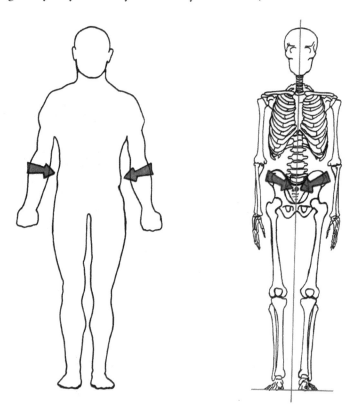

5. Assumption: The spine is on the back. In reality, the tips of the dorsal processes of your vertebrae are on your back. However, the spinal column itself (made up of the vertebral bodies) is more centrally located.

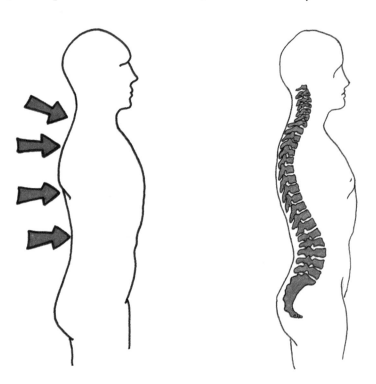

6. Assumption: The legs attach below the center of the body. In reality, your legs attach at the hip joint. This is where the bone-to-bone connection is. Notice how close it is to the body's center of gravity.

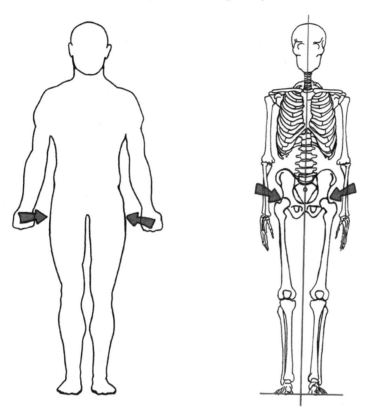

7. Assumption: The femurs (thighbones) are straight. In reality, femurs (thighbones) are reminiscent of the arched beam of a flying buttress (notice the top of the femur).

8. Assumption: The knees bend just above the knee cap. In reality, your knees bend below the kneecaps.

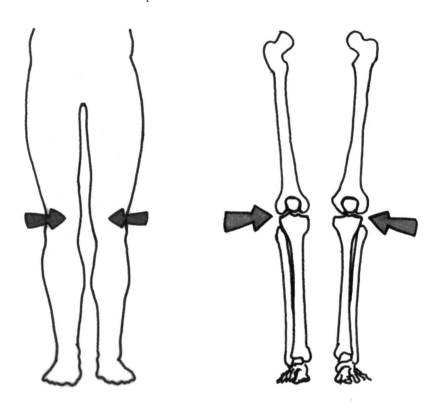

9. Assumption: The feet are L-shaped. In reality, your feet are not just in front of your legs; the heels are behind your ankles. Your feet are balanced like a tripod.

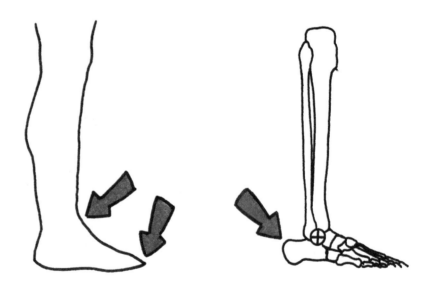

Misconceptions Influence Movement   The misconceptions in the preceding list may seem logical, or they may at least seem to fit in with your general perception of your body. It is interesting to note how often these ideas correspond to clothing: that is, your neck is from your collar to your chin; your arm attaches at the seam of your shirt; your feet are shaped like socks; and so on.

However, although these assumptions are not totally wrong in every case, they're not exactly accurate either.

These seemingly innocuous generalizations can influence how you visualize moving. For example, to a certain extent, your golf swing comes from where you think your arms attach or from where and how you think your hips move.

If you want to allow joints to be available, knowing where they really are versus having a general idea of where you *think* they are will make learning and improving your performance easier no matter what you are doing—getting out of a chair, raking the leaves, acting, doing yoga, or hitting a tennis ball.

If you can envision your body and how it is designed to move, you will at the very least be informed. You will have a mental picture of your body that is in harmony with the natural design.

Being aware of these misconceptions and having a revised mental picture of your body's structure may help you move your body more efficiently and thereby increase the effectiveness of your practice sessions.

Your movements, as you practice or perform, will become more efficient because you will be working with the natural design for movement. You will not be working against yourself.

It is interesting to note that when people have movement problems, they are usually given exercises to correct the problem. But unless you change how you move while performing the correcting exercises, you will do the exercises using the same movement pattern that caused the problem in the first place.

Muscles

A discussion of the dynamic working of the body is not complete without a description of how the muscles affect movement. George B. Bridgman's description of the relationship between our muscles and the movements they perform is valuable here: "Muscles express also laws of leverage; they are large in proportion to the length of the lever they move. Those of the individual fingers are small and can fit in between the bones of the hand. They grow larger as we ascend the arm, the leverage being longer and the weight greater. The muscles of the forearm are larger than those of the fingers; those of the arm larger than those of the forearm, while the muscles of the shoulder are larger still" (*Constructive Anatomy*).

How Muscles Work

If you think back to your high school biology class, you'll remember that muscles can do three things: they can contract, they can stretch, and they can maintain volume. Muscles cannot push.

In order for a body part to move efficiently, one muscle contracts while the opposing muscle relaxes and lengthens. When you make the opposite movement, the roles of the muscles reverse. However, it is also true that a joint can move if opposing muscles contract. It's just that cocontraction is not efficient.

This illustration shows the biceps muscle stretching as the triceps muscle contracts in the drawing on the left. In the drawings on the right, the biceps contracts as the triceps stretches.

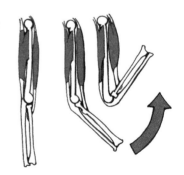

Muscular movement is a balance between stretching and contracting, with skeletal muscles working in pairs.

When we tighten to move, often the unconscious choice is to contract not only the contracting muscles (flexors) but also the stretching muscles (extensors).

This action or choice makes you feel like you are stable. But in reality, you have opted for a static construct that impedes the efficiency of your body.

In a balanced body, when flexors flex, the extensors extend.

—IDA P. ROLF

Muscles Span Joints

Remember, muscles span joints. When you tighten muscles unnecessarily for what you think is better control or to "do a good job," you are interfering with a natural process and limiting movement by locking or holding your joints. In tai chi, the joints are called "the energy gates of the body." This means that if your joints are locked, so is your energy.

If muscles didn't overlap joints, you couldn't move. Yet, as I discussed in chapter 2, most people conceive of the body as parts, an assumption that separates and compartmentalizes the body at the joints.

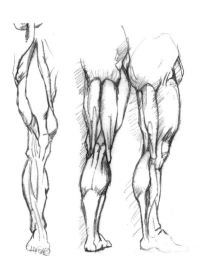

I believe this is one of the reasons why people tend to hold joints still when they want to move "one part" (like holding an elbow joint to move the arm).

Most of us are familiar with the biceps muscle and know where the body of the biceps is (in the front of the upper arm). Did you know that the biceps muscle attaches both below the elbow and above the shoulder joint?

Thinking of your arm as including muscles that overlap the joints can make a real difference in how you envision moving your arms. In this illustration, you can see how the muscles of the arm span the joints.

Muscles Need to Engage—Not Tighten

When we perform or make any movement, we want to allow the torso to retain suspension. We want to remain soft and supple and to be available to expand and contract when we breathe and when we move our arms and legs.

We've noted that when most people move an arm, for example, they make the assumption that they have to stabilize the torso to counteract the weight shift, and then they tighten to initiate the arm movement.

Of course, as I've already noted, muscles must engage for you to move against gravity. But it's possible to use your weight to your advantage so that you don't have to first tighten in order to move. Remember, tightening requires more effort than allowing the whole body to work together.

Redefining Body Parts

If you redefine the parts of the body by the muscles that move them, you will get a very different picture of your body and a different conception of how you look and how you move. For example, thinking of the foot as a body part that ends at your ankle is very different from thinking of it as flowing into your leg.

The muscles of your feet are more extensive than you might think at first. They span the area from the foot itself to just below the knee on the front and to just above the knee on the back, as shown in these illustrations below.

YOUR LEGS

If we define a leg by the muscles that move the leg, we get a larger picture. In addition to other leg muscles, our redefined view of the front should include the iliacus (pelvic) muscle and the psoas muscle.

The psoas is the innermost muscle of the leg and is a hip flexor. As shown here, it resembles suspenders that connect your spine to the femur.

In your torso, the psoas attaches to the sides of your lumbar vertebrae at the twelfth rib, crosses over the pelvis, and attaches to your leg at the lesser trochanter of your femur (a small bony bump that is located on the inside of the femur, toward the top), as shown in the illustration to the left.

Note that muscles of the upper leg attach below the knee, just as muscles of the upper arm attach below the elbow.

From the front, our redefined leg would now look like the illustration to the right.

For the top and rear of the leg, we have to include the gluteus maximus, the largest muscle of the body, known for giving shape to the buttocks.

So from the rear, the redefined leg would now look like these illustrations.

YOUR HANDS

Your hands would actually start above your elbow if you included all related muscles. Your redefined arms and hands would look like the following illustration.

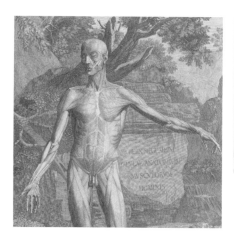
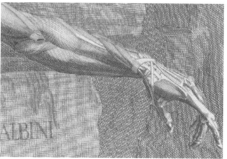

YOUR ARMS

On the back of your body, your redefined arm includes a muscle called the latissimus dorsi (which means "widest back"), which spans from T7 (thoracic vertebra 7) all the way down to your sacrum, plus the trapezius muscle, which extends from the back of your head all the way to the bottom of your rib cage.

On the front of your body, your pectoralis major attaches to your collarbone and to the side and a bit below the sternum, making your redefined arm look like this illustration.

THE NECK AND BEYOND

If all the muscles involved in neck movement were considered, your neck, on the back, would be extensive, as shown in this illustration.

If we include the trapezius muscle, then the most external muscles of the neck actually extend all the way down to your twelfth rib. They also drape out to the shoulders on the back, reminiscent of a medieval hood, as shown below.

On the front, the head and neck muscles extend down at least to the collarbone.

The deep inner anterior (front) muscles of the neck (including the longus colli) actually reach down inside the chest cavity to the third thoracic vertebra.

Now the questions arise: *What is the neck? What is the torso?* Some muscles are both neck and torso; they are shared. The trapezius is neck, arm, and torso.

The Body as One Muscle

In the final analysis, we realize that we don't have parts as we originally thought of them. We have patterns that interrelate with multiple functions. The body is all one.

If you want to increase your capacity for expression and/or improve the efficiency of your movement, you must allow the muscles of your body to move as one: one muscle with more than six hundred compartments.

In terms of thinking about how you move, it is probably more useful not to think of having arms, legs, and so on at all but just to have a pure intention.

A Metaphor for the Body

In the following exercise, the hand is meant to serve as a metaphor for the whole body. It is part of the "body mapping" concept of Alexander Technique teachers Barbara and Bill Conable. They have written extensively on this method of sorting out assumptions about movement. Bill Conable illustrated this point with the following demonstration. By doing this awareness study, you will see how assumptions can affect how you move.

You will appreciate the importance of having an accurate picture of how the parts of the body fit together. You will also see how your understanding of those relationships could affect how you move and your potential for improvement.

AWARENESS STUDY: Identifying the Joints of the Hand

1. Turn your right hand so that the palm faces up, as in this illustration.

2. With the index finger of your left hand, point to the first joint from the tip of the index finger of your right hand.

   Most people point to the area to which the arrow points in the following illustration.

3. Now point to the second joint from the tip of your index finger.

   Most people point to the area to which the arrow points in the following illustration.

4. Point to the third joint from the tip of your index finger.

   Most people point to the area to which the arrow points in the following illustration.

5. Now move your hand in a gripping motion as if the joint was really there, located at the crease at the base of your fingers.

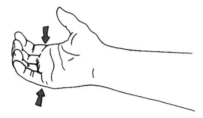

6. Hold your finger at this third crease. You will notice that there is no joint located there.

   The joint is actually one crease lower, as shown below.

7. Attempt to move your finger from where the *imaginary* third joint is, and then move it from where the third joint *really* is. You'll find that you experience two very different movement patterns.

   The first pattern will seem compressive or congested, and the second will feel more spacious and will consequently take less force. Most people discover that it takes a lot less effort to move from where the joint really is.
   You may even notice that the shape of the hand actually seems to change as you explore the different patterns. The same is true of the body as a whole.

The Dynamic Body and Expression

If you study the dynamic model of the body that is described in this chapter, you will have a better appreciation of how the muscles relate to the skeleton and how the body moves in patterns rather than parts.
   This knowledge will help you find greater expression in your movement in everyday life and when performing.

Chapter 7

The Foot

In all positions, the foot tends to keep itself flat with the ground; the arches of the foot changing accordingly.

—GEORGE B. BRIDGMAN,
Constructive Anatomy

As you move, your foot is meant to be dynamic, soft, and in contact with the earth. Your ankle is also meant to be dynamic, constantly adjusting to the shifting forces and weight of the body above it, allowing balance and counterbalance and flow with an economy of force. Famed actor Sir Laurence Olivier is quoted as saying that the secret of acting is to have "soft feet" (*On Acting*).

Dynamic Structure of the Foot and Ankle

When you are standing, every movement and every shift in weight necessitates movement in your ankle. At the same time, the adjustment is transferred into the foot. It is part of the total pattern for efficient motion.

If there is tension in your foot and/or ankle, rest assured that there is a corresponding compensatory pattern of tension somewhere else in the rest of your body. The foot's job is to relate to the terrain. To accomplish this task, the joints of the ankle and foot need to be available, which means your feet need to be relaxed.

The Foot Structure

When you jump, there is a great deal of stress (pounds per square inch) directed into your foot. If your foot were a single bone, all that stress directed onto a single bone would cause it to shatter at the time of impact.

In order to absorb this stress, your foot is made of several bones and flexible arches. The foot is dynamic: it flexes under the load. When the downward forces are applied, they are distributed across a larger area

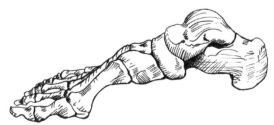

over the multiple bones of the foot. Stanislavski is reported as saying that "a flexible foot and toes are the basis of lightness of walking" (Stanislavski and Pavel Rumyantsev, *Stanislavski on Opera*).

YOUR FOOT AS TRIPOD

Your foot has a design similar to a tripod. This tripod, which has three primary points of contact with the terrain (where most of the contact forces are concentrated), is an inherently stable construct.

With four points of contact (like a table), it is possible for one point not to be touching the terrain—say, on an uneven surface. But with three points of contact (like a music stand or camera tripod), all three points will make contact with the terrain. The tripod design is stable. The three contact points of the foot are the ball of the big toe, the ball of the little toe, and the heel. (The illustration of the foot at left is shown from the bottom, while the skeletal foot is shown from above.)

THE ARCHES

Connecting the three points of the foot's tripod are three arches.

1. The weight-bearing arch connects the ball of the big toe to the heel.
2. The balance arch, or outside arch, connects the ball of the little toe to the heel.
3. The transverse arch connects the ball of the big toe and the ball of the little toe.

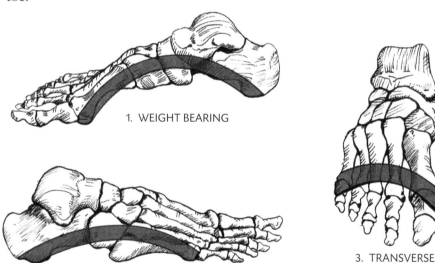

1. WEIGHT BEARING

2. BALANCE

3. TRANSVERSE

With its arches and flexibility, the foot is designed to absorb shock and adapt to uneven surfaces, whether the ground you're traversing is rocky or flat.

Most people think of the foot as being located in front of the leg. They don't consider that the leg, as we've discussed in earlier chapters, is actually located on top of the foot, with the heel behind the ankle, as shown in this illustration.

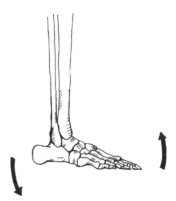

This design allows opposition when you move your foot: the heel pivots one way as the toe of the foot pivots in the opposite direction.

Weight Distribution

The foot is designed so that the weight of the body is distributed over the whole foot, with roughly 50 percent of your weight on your toes and 50 percent on your heels.

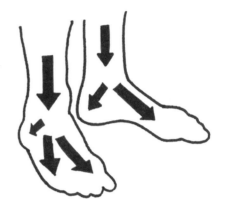

Carrying a disproportionate amount of your weight on the front part of the foot or on your heel causes compensations throughout the rest of the body.

The Tracking of the Foot

If we took your feet into the "foot alignment shop," we would find that the foot is meant to track (align) along a line that extends from the heel through a point between the second and third toe, as seen in the following illustration.

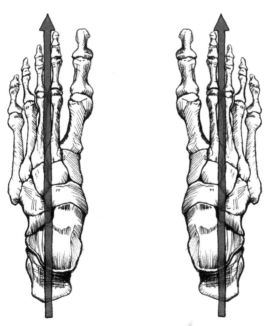

This line will become important when we consider the movement of the foot in relation to the entire leg. If there were a generalized assumption about tracking, I think most people would erroneously assume that the line goes *through* the big toe.

On top of the foot's tripod is your talus bone (the center part of the ankle). If we draw lines from the individual points of the tripod, at the apex is the talus.

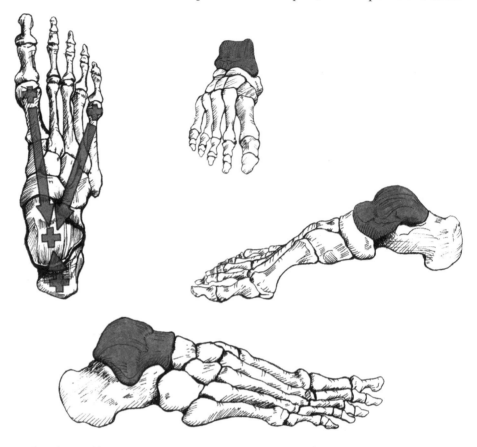

(In the above illustration, the foot at the top left is shown from above, with arrows pointing from the three points of the tripod to the top of the talus bone. The other drawings are views of the foot from various angles; in each one, the talus bone is shaded.)

What we commonly call the ankle is actually parts of three bones: the talus bone, plus the bottom of the tibia and the bottom of the fibula (the lower leg bones). The bony bumps on each side of what we call the ankle joint are actually the bottoms of the tibia and the fibula. The talus bone is between them, as you can see in this illustration.

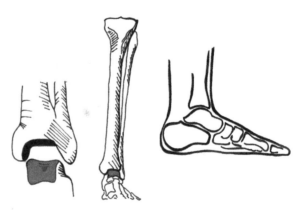

The function of the talus is to distribute the weight of the body and other loads into the entire foot.

The line of balance goes through the ankle joint, where the tibia, fibula, and talus meet. The bottoms of the tibia and fibula form a concave area to match with the rounded top of the talus.

Your entire body balances on top of this dynamic structure.

Standing Up

Isn't it interesting that when most people want to get out of a chair and stand up, one of the first things they do is tighten their feet. Some will grip the floor, and others will actually lift their toes off the ground.

Either choice causes the overall movement pattern to be out of balance and requires more effort. This, in turn, creates the false assumption and the self-fulfilling prophecy that you have to tighten your body to stand up.

Remember, the feet are meant to keep contact with the terrain. They are dynamic, as shown in the following illustration.

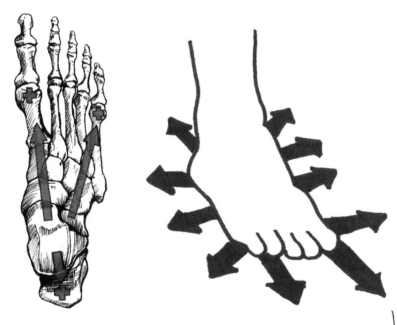

Feet vs. Hands

Put your hands on a table and push down as if you were doing a push-up. As you push, notice that your hands expand on the surface of the table, as shown in this illustration.

In contrast, when people stand up, they usually tighten and grip with their feet. They don't let their feet expand as the weight goes into the floor. There is no downward direction to this movement. It's almost as if they are trying to stand *above* the floor.

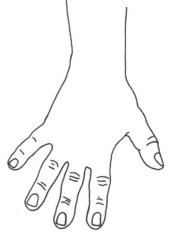

If your hands were feet and you "stood" on them this way, they'd look like this illustration.

Squeeze your fingers and tighten your hand to make it fairly rigid as shown in the drawing, then push down. How does it feel? How does your capacity for expression feel?

Tightened Feet

The feet are designed to be flexible. Yet the idea of a flexible, soft foot (not a locked foot) may seem almost counterintuitive.

In my workshops, I'll sometimes ask a participant to lean back while I support his or her weight. Most people will immediately tighten their feet and ankles, making them rigid, and their feet will leave the floor, as shown in this illustration.

The only way to become more stable is to allow your foot to be in contact with the floor.

Flexible Foot

Tension in the foot lessens the amount of surface area in contact with the floor. It is inefficient and a waste of energy. The idea of a flexible foot is the foundation for balanced dynamic posture and motion. Sir Laurence Olivier's assessment was correct: soft, flexible feet are the secret to a successful performance.

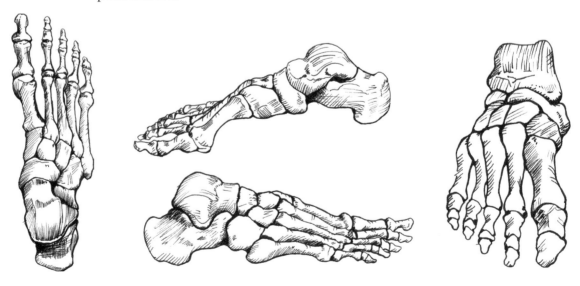

1. To simulate foot tension, stand and lift all ten of your toes off the ground and keep them elevated.
2. Now wave your arms at random through a large range of movement.

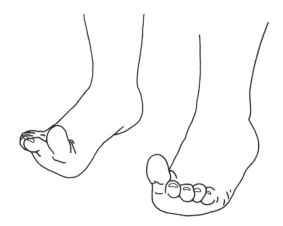

I think the point has been made: any tension in the feet and ankles will affect how you move your arms. Foot tension includes any gripping, tightening, holding of any kind, and/or excessive rotation onto the outer or inner arches of the foot.

Flexing the Foot

Think about how you would flex your foot if you were sitting in a chair with your leg out in front of you.

Most people conceive of flexing the foot as the movement made by pulling the toes and the front part of the foot back toward their torso. The typical move is shown in the illustration on the left.

In reality, when you flex your foot, and the toes come up and back toward you, your heel actually moves down and away from you, as shown in the illustration on the right.

In the same way, when your heel comes toward you, the toes move away.

That is what we mean by allowing opposition—a theme that is repeated over and over again in the body. Opposition allows a movement to take less effort.

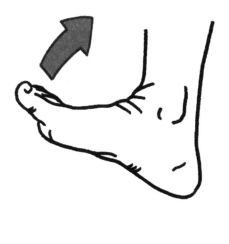
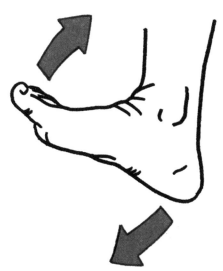

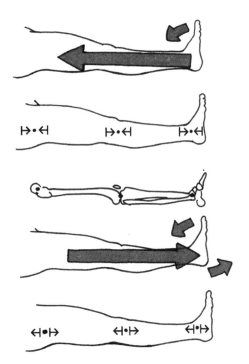

Creating Opposition

In my classes, I use an exercise to illustrate the way in which allowing opposition takes less effort. I create the opposition of the foot-flexing motion for a student. To do so, I pull on the student's heel while he or she is lying on the floor.

As the foot is flexed, the student is amazed to see the shape of the leg change.

When the student pulls the toes back without allowing the heel to move away, there is compression in the hip, knee, and ankle joints, as shown in the top two drawings in this illustration.

In contrast, when I pull on the heel, there is expansion in all the joints, even though the toes are still moving back toward the body, as illustrated in the bottom two drawings in the illustration.

Compression and Expansion

As shown in the preceding exercise, the way you flex your foot can actually change the shape of your thigh and the action of your entire leg. When you allow opposition, the leg seems to get longer, and the hip area relaxes. There is expansion in the leg (instead of compression), and moving the leg feels lighter and easier.

If you conceptualize flexing the foot as bringing the toes toward you without allowing opposition, there is actually less movement than when you allow the heel to move away from you. Your whole leg, including the quadriceps muscles, will probably tighten up in order to accomplish this movement. As a result, the movement feels congested.

Blocking oppositional movement requires more effort than letting movement happen. Because muscles span joints, excess effort tends to squeeze the joint. In other words, blocking oppositional movement causes compression, while allowing oppositional movement allows expansion.

Summary

There are three things to remember about foot movement:

Keep the foot flexible.
Allow the entire foot to be in contact with the terrain.
Take advantage of opposition.

Whether you are in a movement class (e.g., yoga), playing a sport, performing in a play, or just getting out of a chair, these concepts are the key to having soft feet that aid in efficient movement and in creating a successful, expressive performance.

Chapter 8
The Knee

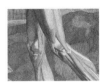

As we move upward from the foot and ankle, the lower leg bones lead us directly to the knee. Let's take a look at this important joint.

Lower Leg Bones

There are two bones in the lower leg: the tibia (the large, inner bone) and the fibula (the smaller, outer bone).

At the ankle, both the tibia and the fibula interface with the talus and help provide stability to the ankle.

While the tibia articulates with the upper leg bone (the femur), the fibula does not.

The top of the fibula touches the tibia and assists with the weight-bearing function of the lower leg, but it is not part of the knee joint.

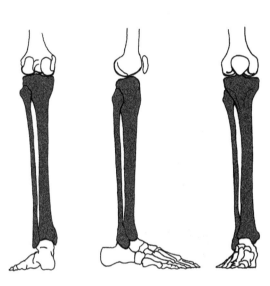

The Knee Joint

The actual knee joint is where the top of your tibia connects with the bottom of your thighbone (the femur). At this juncture, both the tibia and the femur widen. The idea is to provide more surface area, and hence more stability.

The knee joint itself, as Blandine Calais-Germain states in her book *Anatomy of Movement*, is "reminiscent of a rocking chair." The two condyles (rounded protuberances) at the base of the femur resemble the chair's rockers (notice the shaded areas in this illustration). This "rocking chair" rests on the concave surfaces of the tibia (shinbone), as shown in the right drawing.

Attached to the top of the tibia are two C-shaped discs of fibrocartilage (commonly referred to as the meniscus). They help the rocking chair by providing a greater surface area for articulation of the joint, which helps distribute the weight of the upper body onto the lower leg.

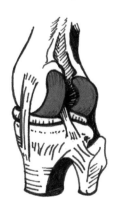

The femur's rocking chair condyles are less curved on the front (which is good for bearing weight) and more curved in the back (which is good for movement).

A Bony Channel

In the middle of the knee is a bony channel between the condyles of the femur, matched by a bony ridge between the indentations on top of the tibia. The cruciate ligaments, which attach to the channel and ridge, help the knee track when you bend it.

You can see this channel and the ridge below it in this illustration of the right knee (viewed from the front).

Asymmetrical Design

The condyles of the femur are not exactly symmetrical.

For our purposes, we'll think of the knee as a simple hinge joint. But in reality, with this unique design, there's more movement in a knee than in a door hinge.

Where the Knee Bends

There is a general misconception about where the knee bends. The knee actually bends just below the kneecap. Most people think of it as bending from slightly above the kneecap.

I was listening to a soccer game the other day, and a player was injured. The announcer said, "I think the injury was below the kneecap." His intent was to imply that it wasn't serious, but that, of course, is right where you wouldn't want the injury to be.

If you think of bending your knee from below the kneecap, not above it, you will find that you can bend your knee with less effort (force).

At the very least, knowing where the knee actually bends will make it easier for you to break your habit of tightening the knees unnecessarily, because you will not be thinking about moving them in the same habitual way.

Knee Ligaments

We often hear of "ACL" injuries, especially in athletes who play such sports as soccer, basketball, tennis, and track, as well as in dancers. The ACL is the anterior cruciate ligament. The posterior cruciate ligament and the ACL are crossed ligaments that attach between the femur's condyles (the "legs" and "rockers" of the "rocking chair"), as seen in the drawing at right below.

On the outside and inside of the knee are two other ligaments, shown in the top drawing here.

These ligaments are the medial (tibial) collateral ligament, which runs on the inside of the knee, and the lateral (fibular) collateral ligament, which runs on the outside of the knee.

Twisting the knee too far or too abruptly can cause the ACL or one of the other ligaments to tear.

The Knee While Standing

There are two common choices people tend to make with regard to movement of the knee, and both are static: hyperextending and overbending.

Some people tend to lock the knee so that it is hyperextended (pushed too far back), as shown in this illustration. This is inefficient, as it is a waste of energy and interrupts the flow of movement through the legs. It also impedes the ability to balance.

The opposite choice is to keep the knees bent slightly, as in the following illustration. This choice, overbending, is also inefficient. Although keeping the knees slightly bent while moving is good, standing with bent knees for a long period of time increases stress by putting more force on less surface area. Over time, this could cause damage to your knee.

Bent knees often result when people notice that they are pushing forward through their lower backs. This knee bending can help them release the pushing in their lower backs, but this is a quick fix and avoids the real issue of why they are pushing in the lower back in the first place.

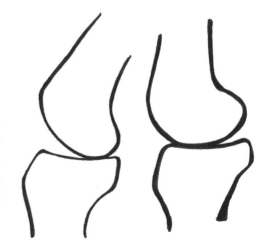

Overbent and hyperextended knees are the extremes of knee movement. Neither is the balanced choice.

The efficient choice is not to hyperextend or overbend the knees while standing but simply to let the femur balance on top of the tibia. If you are accustomed to locking your knees, you will notice that your knees feel more dynamic when you simply allow the leg bones to balance, one on top of the other. You'll also find that movement flows through your body much more easily.

Moving the Knee

Many movements require bending the knee: sitting, getting out of a chair, climbing stairs, and so on. For these movements, most people tighten their knees in order to move their legs. But you don't need to tighten, stiffen, and/or hold your knees as you stand or sit.

AWARENESS STUDY: Raising the Knee

1. As you sit in your chair, raise your knee about six inches.

The muscles engage in order to move. But if you're like most people, you probably also first tighten your knee in order to create that movement. (You can demonstrate this to yourself by noticing that after you lift your leg, the lower leg remains in the same angle that it was in before you moved it.) That tightening is completely unnecessary.

2. See if you can move your knee with less tightening.

Let the lower leg move as the weight shifts. In other words, let it hang instead of retaining the old angle. When you pause to think about it, you will be able to make this movement using less force.

Summary

The knee is a hingelike joint that bends where the femur and the tibia come together, below the kneecap. Try not to grip or hold your knees when you perform. Allowing the knee joint to be available promotes greater balance, requires less force, and permits more expressive flow.

Chapter 9
The Thigh

The upper leg bone, or thigh, is called the femur. This is a slightly curved bone, shaped, as noted in chapter 6, something like the arched beam of a flying buttress.

Femur Anecdote

Imagine this scene: An actress, a member of an English Shakespearean acting company, pulls bones out of a burlap bag that she's been carrying around. She then assembles a skeleton on the stage floor. She places the femurs (thighbones) upside down.

I think I know why. Perhaps it's because, like most people, the actress thinks thighbones are straight—as illustrated in the section on misconceptions in chapter 6. Therefore, the only way her idea of a thighbone can mesh with the real shape of the thighbone (shown again in the illustration below) is for her to put the femurs upside down and sideways.

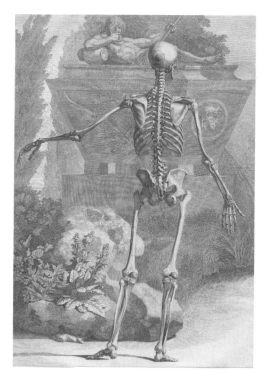

The Femur's Shape

To be sure you are clear about the shape of the femur, illustrations are repeated here, including both a reference illustration of the pelvis showing the top curved portion of the femur (thighbone) and two front views of the right femur.

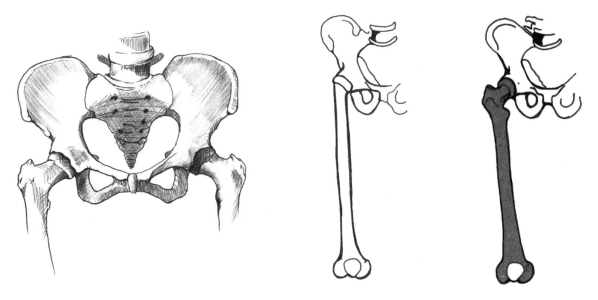

The line drawing shows how people think of the femur as a straight bone.

The shaded drawing shows the femur as it really is, with its curved arch (like a flying buttress) at the top.

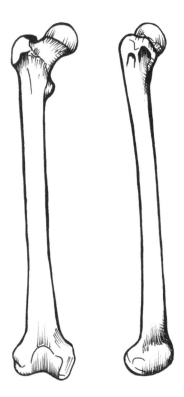

Benefits of the Femur's Curve

As I've just noted and as you can see in this front and side view of the right femur, the femur is not straight. It is slightly curved, with a ball-shaped protrusion (the head) at the top and a large projection of bone (the greater trochanter) and smaller projection (the lesser trochanter) beneath the neck.

The femur's shape allows the head to insert into the hip joint from the side. This relationship between the femur and the hip joint has the following advantages:

1. It makes the hip more stable, because the femur is not easily pushed away from the hip joint.
2. It provides the hip muscles with a lever, which increases the mechanical efficiency of the leg. (Movement doesn't require as much effort.)
3. It allows for opposition, by creating a counterbalancing movement.

If the femurs were straight, then, as the weight of the body was transferred onto them, the force would push them out, away from the hip joint, as shown on the left in the next illustration.

However, as shown on the right in the drawing, due to the femur's curved shape, the downward force of the body's weight on the ball-shaped head causes movement around the femur's little neck and pushes the femur in, toward the hips, thus stabilizing the hip joint, in the same way a flying buttress stabilizes a cathedral.

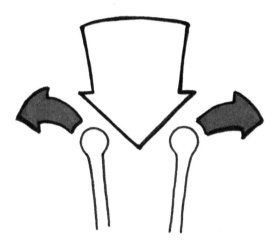

Leverage

To demonstrate leverage, I ask a student to sit and cross his or her legs. Then I put an entire leg-and-foot section of a skeleton right on the student's top leg. I ask the student to place a thumb and index finger on the shaft of the femur and try to swing the skeletal foot from side to side, noticing how much effort it takes.

I then have the student place his or her fingers at the top of the femur, and I ask the student to again swing the foot of the skeleton from side to side, using the femur's neck as a lever. The student is amazed at how much easier it is to move the leg and foot using this little bit of leverage.

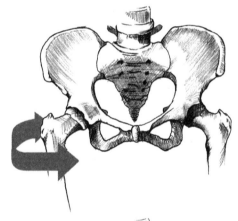

The following concept may be a little hard to figure out at first, because we don't think about this movement. But let's give it a try.

You are looking at the pelvis and the hip joints. If you were standing and facing the page, this would be your hip viewed from the front.

The arrow illustrates the movement of the femur when you are rotating your leg so that the hip is "open" (external rotation) or rotating the leg so that the hip is "closed" (internal rotation).

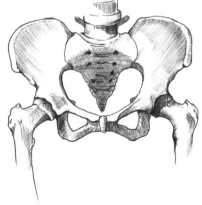

Notice how the neck of the femur creates more movement. If the femur were merely straight, your leg would only rotate around the axis of the ball. This little lever, the neck of the femur, reduces the amount of muscular force required to move your leg.

Opposition

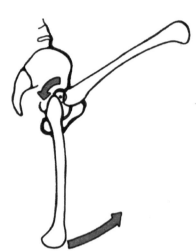

When you lift a knee (e.g., in the movement you might make if you were marching), there is a counterbalancing movement with the greater trochanter (the large projection at the top of the femur).

This opposition in the femur is similar to the movement that happens when flexing the foot: when the toes go up, the heel goes down. With the femur, as the right knee moves upward, as shown in this illustration, the greater trochanter moves downward.

The opposition of the greater trochanter and lower femur allows for a slight counterbalancing action and lets the movement be more expansive.

Location of the Femur

Another thing to note about thighbones is that when you sit, they are lower than you might think. When I ask seated students where their femurs are, most of them put their hands on the top surface of their thighs.

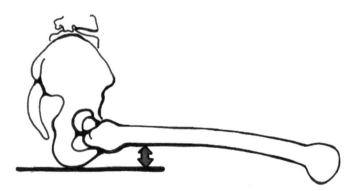

However, if you are sitting, your thighbones are just above your chair, as shown in this illustration.

If you wedge your hand between the chair and your leg, you'll feel how close the femur is to the back of leg.

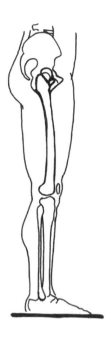

In a similar manner, when you stand, your femur is farther back than most people assume, as shown in this illustration.

Being aware of this fact helps you understand where the weight of the body when standing is transferred through your thigh. You are balancing farther back than you might at first think.

Flexibility Note

When you initiate the movement of lifting your knee by tensing and compressing your hip and knee joints, you are, in effect, also lifting the weight of the torso, as shown by the arrows in the illustration below.

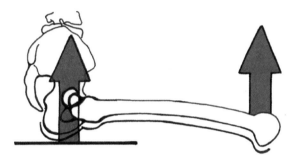

(This movement is very habituated, and it may take a bit of experimenting to be able to notice it by yourself. To figure it out, you may have to put your fingers underneath your sit bones—the broadened bony areas at the base of the pelvis that you sit on. Remember, the first bump you feel on the outside of your leg is not the sit bone. It is the greater trochanter of the femur. Your sit bones are further underneath you.)

In contrast, when you lift your knee with your hip joint open and available, you allow the weight of the torso to transfer to the chair, as shown by the large arrow in the next illustration.

With this movement, it is much easier to lift your knee. The idea of keeping your hip and leg joints available is extremely important for performers who perform while sitting. With ease of movement comes greater flexibility. If you are an instrumentalist, sitting this way will affect the sound of your instrument.

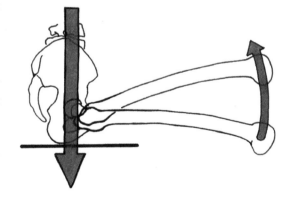

Summary

The curved thighbone, the femur, aids in stability, contributes to the efficiency of the leg's movement, and allows for counterbalance. Ease of movement in the hip joint results in greater flexibility.

Chapter 10
The Leg

Now that we've discussed the foot, knee, and thigh, let's consider the entire leg.

Misconception about the Leg

Most people's conception of the leg is that it stops where it meets the torso.

This seems logical enough. If you are sitting and you look down, you see your legs in front of your torso, as shown in the cartoon to the left. If you bend a little further forward and look at your feet, you see your feet in front of your legs.

Perhaps that's why most people don't consider how much of the leg they are sitting on—just as they don't consider that the heel is behind the bones of the lower leg.

However, as pointed out before, the muscles of the buttocks are part of the total leg. Therefore, you could conclude that when you sit, you are actually sitting *on top* of your legs, not behind them.

Leg Movement

When you are standing, the three major joints of the leg (the hip, the knee, and the ankle) form a vertical line, as shown here. (Actually, if you want to be absolutely precise, the line formed by connecting these joints is about three degrees from vertical.)

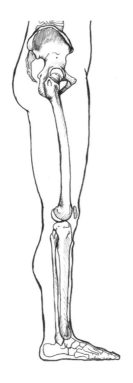  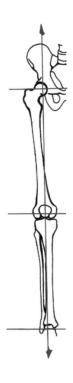

When you bend your knee and move your bent leg from side to side, the leg moves or pivots from the hip joint. Remember, the knee is a simple hinge, and it can't swing sideways.

The point is that the leg moves from the hip. The inefficient habit most people have is to hold the knee still when they want to move their leg. All this habit does is cause you to tighten your knee unnecessarily.

Clarification

Saying that movement of the leg originates at the hip joint does not mean that the only "correct" way to stand is to have both feet parallel and to not allow any movement in the knee or ankle. However, if, for example, you have a foot turned to the side, the movement isn't just in your foot. There is movement in your whole leg, and that turning out is designed to originate in your hip.

Tracking of Knee and Foot

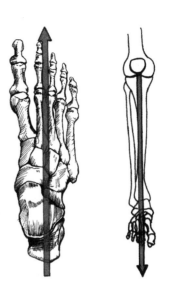

As discussed in chapter 7, a line drawn from the heel of the foot to a point between the second and third toe marks the tracking line of the foot.

Generally speaking, your knee follows the tracking line of the foot, as shown in the drawing at the right in this illustration.

An example of alignment of the knee and foot is what happens when you squat: your kneecaps are in line with the tracking line of your foot and do not extend to the right or left of the foot.

Compensation and Leg Tracking

As discussed in chapter 4, people often stand with the pelvis thrust forward. With the pelvis forward, they also often stand with their feet rotated out to the sides, because it is a more comfortable position. This is commonly referred to as a "ducklike" stance.

Rotating the feet out to the sides is a compensation for the pelvis being forward. If your pelvis isn't forward, you don't need or want to rotate your feet to the sides. At the same time, if your feet are parallel, so that your legs track with the feet, you don't need or want to thrust your pelvis forward.

AWARENESS STUDY: Compensation and Tracking

1. Rotate your feet outward, then push your pelvis forward.
2. Put your feet parallel, then push your pelvis forward.

You'll find that pushing your pelvis forward isn't as comfortable without the "ducklike" compensation.

Leg Tracking While Sitting

Tracking isn't just tightening the feet and turning them so they are straight. The joints need to be dynamic.

To be sure that your legs and feet track while you're sitting, try picking up your leg by placing your hands just at the back of the knee and lifting. Then let the lower leg relax, and lower the foot back onto the floor. Most people will find that their foot is now tracking or at least is a lot closer to tracking than it had been.

If there was no change in the position of your foot after you tried the preceding movement, it means that you have not yet gained sufficient awareness to allow your lower leg and foot to relax. Wiggle your foot around a bit, shake it, and try it again. If it still doesn't track, give it a little more time.

Allowing the feet and legs to track is especially important for instrumentalists when they perform sitting down. They can instantly improve the resonance of their instruments simply by letting their feet align with their knees.

AWARENESS STUDY: Performing While Sitting

1. Sit down.
2. Rotate your feet outward to the "ducklike" position, then wave your arms.
3. Let your feet track, then wave your arms.
4. Notice the difference. Obviously the "ducklike" feet block movement.

The Hip Joint

The hip joint is where the mobility of the leg really is. In contrast the tripod of the foot is meant to adjust to the terrain, and the knee is a simple hinge joint that bends in relation to the foot.

To locate your hip joints, rest your hands on your waist. You'll feel two bony points at the front and top of your pelvis—what we commonly call your hipbones. Just a little below these bony points is roughly where your hip joints are.

On the side of your leg, the bony bumps that you feel are actually the trochanters, and just above the top of the trochanters and closer to your center is the level of the hip joint.

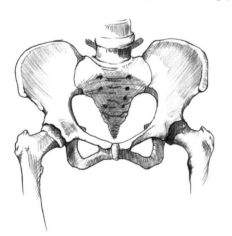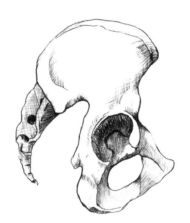

The first drawing of the illustration shows the pelvis (viewed from the front) and the trochanters at the top of the femurs.

The other drawings are side views of the pelvis, with the person's front toward the right of the page. These drawings show the relationship between the pelvis and the right hip joint.

Relation of Femur to Hip Joint

The femur (your thighbone) extends from the knee to the hip joint, but not in a perfectly straight line.

The greater trochanter (the large protrusion at the top of the femur) extends to the outside of the line connecting the hip, knee, and ankle, as shown in this illustration.

It is important that when you visualize the hip joint, you allow for the space created by the neck of the femur. Assuming that your thighbones are straight and that they insert straight into your hip joint will most likely limit your movement.

Movement of the Upper Leg

In an earlier exercise, I asked you to sit in a chair and then raise your knee six inches. I noted that tightening the knee is unnecessary for this movement.

The reason tightening the knee is not necessary is that the muscle that *initiates* flexion of the thigh is your psoas, shown in this illustration.

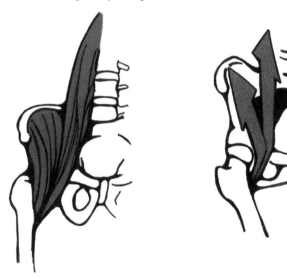

Your thigh's quadriceps muscles engage *after* the psoas initiates the movement in the hip joint and femur.

When you tighten the quads to initiate movement, you are making unnecessary work for yourself. Apart from not being needed and getting in the way of the psoas muscle, the unnecessary quadriceps tightening interrupts the initiating of the movement of the hip joint.

Most people don't even know that they have a psoas muscle. Generally speaking, we are more aware of the muscles on the surface of the body than of the deeper muscles because it is easy for us to feel the surface muscles when they contract.

Summary

For most people, simply getting "soft feet" and not holding in the knees would constitute a major improvement in the efficiency of their overall movement. If they could also allow their hip joints to be available, that would be even better.

Chapter 11
The Torso

Ideally, in reference to gravitation, these blocks [representing the head, chest, and pelvis] would be balanced symmetrically over each other. But rarely in fact, and in action never, is this the case.

In these various movements, the limit is the limitation to movement of the spine. The spine is the structure that connects one part of the body with another. It is a strong column occupying almost the centre or axis of the body.

— GEORGE B. BRIDGMAN, *Constructive Anatomy*

The main part of the body, not including the head, arms, and legs, is the torso. The spine, pelvis, and ribs are the major bone structures of the torso, which contains most of the body's organs.

The entire torso moves as we breathe. As Ida P. Rolf pointed out in her book *Rolfing*, as we inhale, the spine lengthens "from one end to the other"; and as we exhale, the spine shortens.

Significant Points about the Spine

The two most salient points about your spine are

1. the spine is expanding and contracting with every breath and movement;
2. movement happens around your spine, not in front of it.

The spine is the main support of the torso. It is a flexible column made up of a series of graduated bones (vertebrae or vertebral bodies).

Each vertebra is centered over the one beneath it. In between the vertebral bodies are cushioning disks.

There are seven cervical, twelve thoracic, and five lumbar vertebrae, plus the fused five vertebrae of the sacrum, as well as the coccyx, or tailbone.

Movement of the Spine

The movements of the spine are organized one after the other and all at the same time (i.e., they are sequential and simultaneous). As mentioned, in tai chi, there is a metaphor called "moving like a string

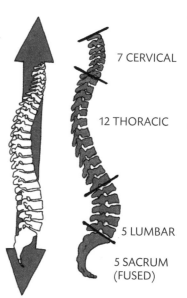

7 CERVICAL

12 THORACIC

5 LUMBAR

5 SACRUM (FUSED)

of pearls," which seems to conjure a helpful image. This metaphor refers to the whole body moving as a series of connected joints.

In the same way, the whole spine moves when you move, with all the joints of the spine being available to your intention. This movement of the spine is designed to happen with every breath and with every movement.

In general, the closer the vertebrae are to your pelvis, the smaller their range of motion is. In the thorax (or chest), you have more movement than in the lower back. The vertebrae of the neck have the greatest range of motion.

If you are standing and look to your right in a movement that involves the entire spine, there will be approximately fifty degrees of rotation in the cervical spine (your head and neck), thirty-five degrees of rotation in the thoracic spine (your chest), and five degrees of rotation in the lumbar spine (lower back).

The Spine's Location in the Torso

When thinking of the spine, most people initially think of the bony bumps on the surface of the back. In reality, these bumps are bony projections that extend backward from the spine itself (your core), which is much more central within the torso, as seen in this illustration.

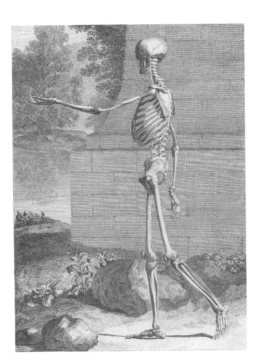
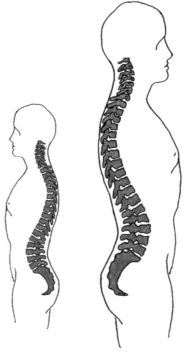

If simplified and looked at from above, your torso would be an oval, and your spine would be a circle inside the oval as seen in the following illustrations. (In each drawing, the back is at the bottom of the oval, and the shaded circle is the spine. The other circles are included to help you understand the spacing.)

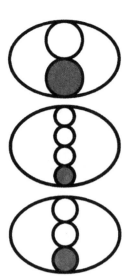

In your lower back, the front of the lumbar spine is in the middle of your body, halfway between the front and back of your lower torso, as shown in the first oval.

In the upper body, the thorax, your spine occupies the back quarter of your torso as shown in the second oval.

As shown in the third oval, your spine occupies the back third of the neck.

The point to be made in the preceding three illustrations is that the spine is much more central than we think. It is also important to point out again that movement happens around the spine, not in front of it.

Flexible Support: Curves of the Spine

As shown in the illustration at left, the spine is not straight. It is a series of curves that allow for greater movement and also for cushioning.

Your spine is curved to absorb shock. If it were straight like a flagpole, the weight and compression you experience when you jump would damage the spine. So you have the curves to absorb shock.

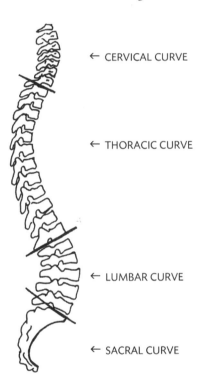

← CERVICAL CURVE

← THORACIC CURVE

There are four curves: the sacral curve, lumbar curve, thoracic curve, and cervical curve. Each backward curve is balanced by a forward curve.

The Vertebrae and Disks

← LUMBAR CURVE

← SACRAL CURVE

As I've noted, the spine is made up of hard vertebrae and softer intervertebral disks (the more elastic tissue between each vertebra).

The vertebrae are the bony parts of the spine. Each vertebra has two parts: the body and the vertebral arch, as seen in the illustration below.

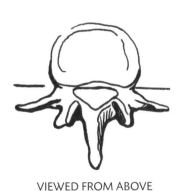

VIEWED FROM ABOVE

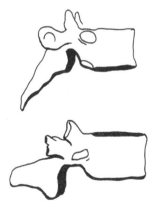

The intervertebral disks are composed of fibrocartilage.

As shown in the cross section below, disks are made up of two parts. The peripheral (or outer) area is called the anulus fibrosus; it looks a bit like cross-hatched slices of onion. The center is the nucleus pulposus; it is ball-like and is composed of a gelatinous substance.

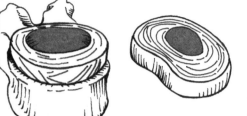

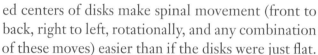

The disks allow much movement between vertebrae. They also allow for shock absorption and weight bearing.

Imagine that there's a ball between every vertebra. The function of the ball is to allow more movement. The round-ed centers of disks make spinal movement (front to back, right to left, rotationally, and any combination of these moves) easier than if the disks were just flat.

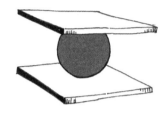

Muscles of the Spine

The muscles of the spine start out very small close to the spinal column itself, spanning first just one or two vertebrae and then three.

Then, outer layers of muscles start connecting larger and larger spans of vertebrae, until a strong core is built up.

Finally, the muscles of the arms and legs are connected with the spine, as are the muscles of respiration. Think of the spine and its musculature as the core of the body.

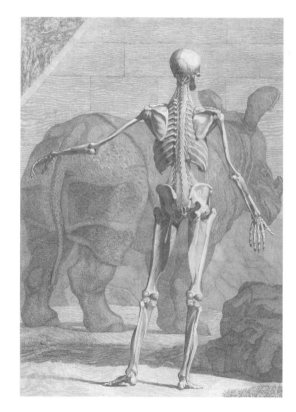

Here's a puzzle for you: if muscles can only stretch and contract (and not push), how does your spine lengthen?

First, imagine the spinal curve of the lower back (the lumbar curve) as a C shape, with the back on the open side of the C, as shown in the illustration on the right.

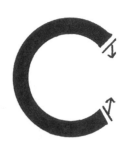

If you connect the two ends of the C with muscles and then contract the muscles, the C will turn into an O as the spine contracts toward the back.

However, if you connect the two ends of the spinal curve by running the muscles on the outside of the C (the front of the spine) and then contract the muscles, the C will turn into an I as the spine contracts toward the front, as illustrated below.

This has the effect of lengthening the spine. It's not only that the spine lengthens; the curves also lessen.

In addition to the muscles on the front and back of the spine, you also have muscles on both sides for balance, expansion and contraction, and stabilization of the spine.

(These illustrations of the spine and its muscles are drawn as if the person is facing the right side of this page.)

The easy way to understand how contracting muscles affect movement of the spine is to remember this formula:

When the muscles in back of the thoracic spine contract, the spine lengthens.
When the muscles in front of the lumbar and cervical spine contract, the spine lengthens.

That's the wonderful thing about the curves of the spine. They allow muscles that can only contract to become "antigravity" muscles. This is how we get from "kidney bean" to "balanced bean" (see chapter 5).

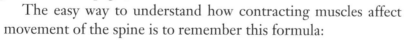

Posture and Support

It is now easy to see how the old view of posture ("Sit up straight and keep shoulders back") is limiting.

The very thought of sitting up straight implies holding yourself and pushing up from the back. With a two-dimensional concept of posture, your support is organized at the back, on the surface of the body. This line of support (on the spine's back side) is out of relation to the line of balance.

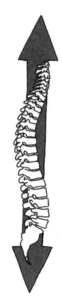

"UP" BECOMES THE PROBLEM

People have this idea that "up straight" is how you are to supposed to hold yourself. Standing or sitting "up" makes you feel as if you are doing a good job with your posture. Although this idea isn't completely wrong, it is not a balanced idea, since there is no "down" included in this thinking.

Unfortunately, most of us try to hold and push ourselves up from the back. This pushing through the back destroys any chance of integrated movement through the spine. It destroys the "string of pearls."

This "up" concept of posture is static, not dynamic. If you are going to push yourself up, you must have some place to push from; and that is the problem. Tightening parts of your body and holding them in order to have a place to push up from cause you to lose flow and balance and require a lot of force.

SUPPORT FROM THE ENTIRE BODY

Your support doesn't come only from your spine. Your support comes from your entire body. It comes from places that maybe you don't even think about.

The volume and weight of your torso and organs help with your support.

Your Spine as a Spring

A long time ago, I saw a picture of myself standing very straight and rigid. When I looked at that picture, I said to myself, "If that's what good posture is, I don't want it." I was stiff and doing what I thought at the time was a very good job.

Then I worked out for myself the idea of the spine being like a spring. When I was in third grade or so, I would take my ballpoint pen apart and take that little spring out. The idea that came to me is that your spine functions like that little spring.

The spring occupies a certain length, which is flexible. It has a capacity for expanding and contracting. The spine is flexible like that spring. There is no need to stretch it up (stand up straight), and you don't have to compress it (slump). You simply let the spine occupy the volume it occupies.

When we look at a baby sitting naturally, we see the most wonderful example of balance through the head and spine.

Like the baby, you don't have to hold yourself "up." Your back can relax. Your spine is flexible support.

The Pelvis

The size of the pelvis is due to its position as the mechanical axis of the body; it is the fulcrum for the muscles of the trunk and legs, and is large in proportion.
—GEORGE B. BRIDGMAN, *Constructive Anatomy*

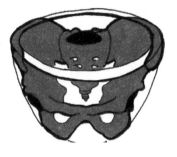

The pelvis is often referred to as the *pelvic bowl.* The word *pelvis* literally means "basin." The contents of your abdominal cavity, the internal organs, rest on and are supported by this bowl.

The pelvic bowl itself is comprised of three pairs of bones: the pubis, ilium, and ischium.

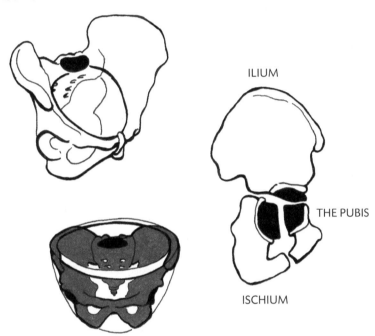

ILIUM

THE PUBIS

ISCHIUM

The sacrum connects the two "halves" of the pelvis in the back, while the front edge of the bowl, above the pubis bone, is filled in by the abdominal wall (soft tissue).

At the base of the pelvic bowl are the ischial tuberosities. When you are sitting, your entire upper body balances on these "rocking chair" bones, which is why the ischial tuberosities are called the "sit bones."

Directions of Movement

On each side of your pelvic bowl is a hip socket, the acetabulum (the name of which means "small bowl" in Latin). The femoral head, the ball on top of your thighbone, fits into the acetabulum. When you are standing, the entire weight of your upper body is balancing on top of these ball-and-socket joints.

The pelvis receives the weight of the upper body and transfers it onto the legs, while it simultaneously absorbs some of the stress of the legs as you run, jump, and so on.

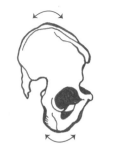

Your pelvis is designed to move in a combination of six directions as you walk: a rocking (1) forward and (2) back, a movement (3) up and (4) down, and a twisting motion (5) right and (6) left.

The Abdominal Cavity

Between the pelvis and the thorax (upper torso) is the abdomen. The abdominal cavity (which I called "the shopping bag" in chapter 3) is filled with organs (which I referred to as "water balloons").

There are three levels, or layers, of muscle that comprise the wall of the abdomen. The most superficial layer of abdominal muscle is what is commonly referred to as your "abs" or "six-pack," the rectus abdominus, which runs vertically.

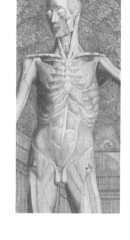

The middle level is made up of two layers of muscle, the external oblique and internal oblique. These muscles run obliquely (at an angle) and could be thought of like the Chinese "handcuffs" that you put your fingers into as a kid and then couldn't get them out. Or perhaps you could just think of them as crosshatched.

The third and innermost layer of abdominal muscle is the transverse abdominus, which runs horizontally.

So you have three layers of muscle: one going up and down, one going diagonally, and one going sideways.

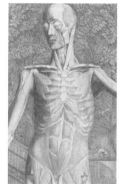

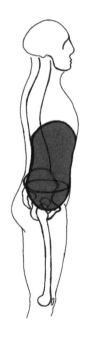

When you move, you are moving the volume and weight of the abdominal cavity, and you are also moving around this volume.

Most of us don't consider moving mass when we move. We naturally relate to the surface of our body, and we look to the surface of the body (specifically the surface of the back) to hold ourselves up.

When we move, thinking of the abdominal cavity as a bag filled with water balloons will help us get a three-dimensional sense of ourselves. As I noted in chapter 3, a three-dimensional conception is essential if we want to move with opposition (allowing counterbalance).

An ancillary benefit to this three-dimensional idea is that it can help us connect with the idea of a lower center of gravity.

The Thorax

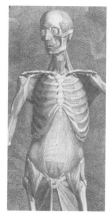

The thorax is the upper part of the body between the neck and diaphragm and includes the thoracic vertebrae, the ribs, and the sternum (breastbone), as well as the organs of the upper body.

The Ribs

If you ask people where their ribs are, most will tell you that the ribs are at their sides, just above their waist. Given a second's pause, they might add their chest. Very few people would comment that there are ribs right in the armpit, but feel it for yourself.

Hardly anyone would add that while the first rib is located just below the collarbone in the front, it is above your collarbone as you move toward the back.

If you place your fingers just above your collarbone and push in, you'll find your first rib as it curves to the back.

THE RIB CAGE AND ITS STRUCTURE

What an unfortunate metaphor to ascribe to the ribs! The term *cage* doesn't really make one think of movement does it? Yet the rib cage does move, with every breath you take.

The rib cage consists of three types of ribs, the sternum (or breastbone) on the front, and the thoracic vertebrae in the back. Costal cartilage connects the ribs to the breastbone. This cartilage allows elasticity and movement.

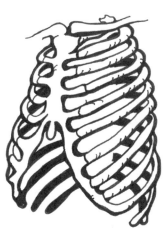

If you look closely at the ribs, you'll notice that some ribs (those at the top of the rib cage) pretty much go right around the body and attach to the breastbone like rings. These are called the "true ribs."

The "false ribs" are the lower ribs that dip below and then join with others at the sternum, sort of like branches of a tree.

At the bottom of the rib cage are two sets of ribs that just float and don't attach to the sternum at all. These are called "floating ribs."

Anatomy books will tell you that the ribs move in a manner similar to the way the handle of a bucket moves, as shown here.

RIB JOINTS

The ribs have several different types of joints, as shown in the illustrations below.

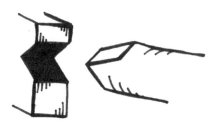

The joint between the cartilage and the breastbone is a chisel-type joint.

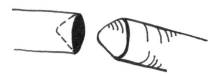

Between the rib and the cartilage is a joint reminiscent of a pencil in a pencil sharpener.

In the back, where the ribs articulate with the vertebrae, the joint simply pivots.

EXTENDING YOUR RANGE OF MOTION

The ribs are connected to the spine and ideally move with the spine.

If your core collapses (i.e., if you slump), so does your chest. Trying to correct a slump by pushing your chest out limits spinal motion. Rather than push the chest out, you want to allow the body to find its own balance.

Unless you allow the ribs to move freely, your spine will not be able to expand and contract with each breath.

When We Breathe

When we breathe, the ribs—in conjunction with the diaphragm (a large muscular partition separating the chest and abdominal cavities)—act as a metaphoric bellows: as the ribs expand, they create a vacuum, and air pressure fills the lungs.

The diaphragm (shown at right on the next page) is located below the lungs, the body's "air balloons," and above the top of the abdominal cavity and its "water balloons."

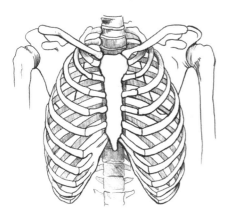

Singers, actors, and musicians who play a wind instrument are familiar with the diaphragm.

When you inhale, the diaphragm contracts. As it contracts, the diaphragm pushes down on the abdominal cavity, which expands outward, changing shape but not volume.

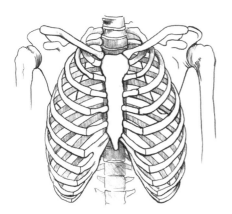
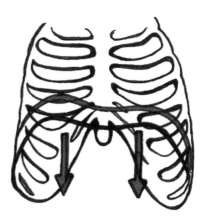

Think of spreading your hands so they represent the diaphragm and then putting them on top of a plastic shopping bag full of water balloons.

If you were to press down, all the spaces between the water balloons would disappear as they were pushed down and out against the sides of the bag. This is similar to what happens in your abdomen when you inhale.

As the diaphragm continues to contract, the lungs are pulled down, and the compressed abdominal cavity acts as a support.

The contracting diaphragm helps lift the ribs up and outward.

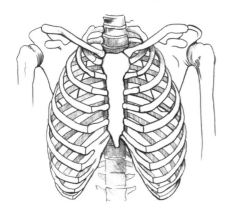
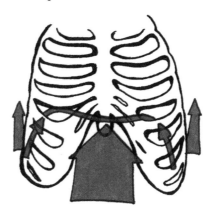

As Ida P. Rolf suggested, the spine goes along for the ride in relation to the movement of the diaphragm: it expands in length as the diaphragm contracts, and it contracts as the diaphragm expands.

Remember (and this is an important point), as the spine lengthens up, the upward movement comes about because the diaphragm is pushing down. That is a definition of opposition: one thing goes up while another counterbalances, going down.

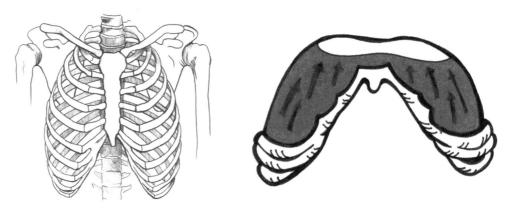

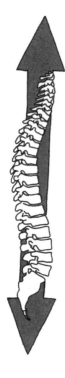

When you exhale, the diaphragm relaxes. The abdominal cavity expands upward, and the air is pushed out. At the same time, the ribs relax, and the spine shortens a little.

Hence we have the movement fundamental I keep repeating: your spine lengthens and contracts with your every breath.

When you breathe, the ribs expand with the inhalation and compress with the exhalation.

Also, the spine extends with the inhalation and shortens a bit with the exhalation, creating a pumping action.

Summary

The body's torso is dynamic. Movement happens around the spine, which is constantly expanding and contracting. When allowed to "move like a string of pearls," the torso amplifies the performer's creative expression.

Chapter 12
The Head and Neck

The education of the actor consists of three parts. The first is the
education of his body, the whole physical apparatus, of every muscle
and sinew. —RICHARD BOLESLAVSKY, *Acting: The First Six Lessons*

The Head and Neck in Balance

It is important for the head to be in balance and supported over the trunk
and vertebral column, so that you can move with a minimal expenditure of
energy (force). As noted in the overture, the head weighs about ten pounds.
Supporting that weight takes much more force when the head is out of balance.

The mother/daughter photos repeated here from the overture illustrate
balance and imbalance of the head over the torso. The mother's head is in front
of her torso, out of balance. The child's head is in balance.

The Head and Neck Joint

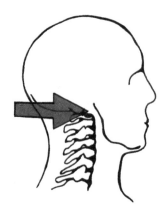

The head and neck joint is located just behind your jaw and right below your ears. Consequently, the head and neck joint is located more centrally, with the neck extending higher, than you might think.

In fact, as noted in chapter 6, by redefining the neck to include the muscles involved in moving the head and neck, we get a very different picture of how extensive the neck is.

Unfortunately, most people have a misconception about the location of the head and neck joint.

As we've already noted, many people say that the neck attaches to the head at the back, as shown in the illustration on the right.

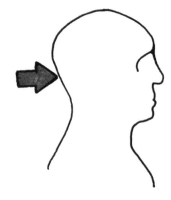

Similarly, when many people look at themselves in the mirror, they view the neck as extending from just above the shoulders (where it attaches to the torso) to below the chin, as shown below.

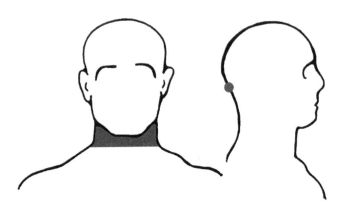

Of course, the combined concepts don't work. You can't have your neck below your chin and the attachment above it at the back of the head. Once you grasp this discrepancy, it is easier for you to visualize the neck as described at the beginning of this section.

Advantage of Head and Neck Joint's Location

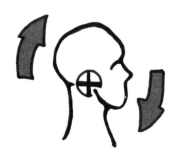

An advantage of the actual location of the head and neck joint is that it affords opposition of movement: when your nose goes down, the back of your head goes up, and when your nose goes to the left, the back of the head goes to the right. The movement is balanced.

Changing the pattern of movement can help erase some of the holding patterns that have become habits for us. The following awareness study shows how this works with the head and neck.

AWARENESS STUDY: Changing the Pattern by Thinking about It Differently

1. Look to the right.

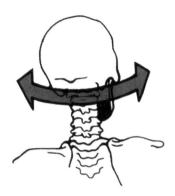

2. Now, instead of "looking to the right," move the back of your head to the left.

You will notice that the second movement feels easier.

By moving the back of your head to the left, you found a new pattern to replace your old inefficient habitual pattern of tightening the joints and muscles in order to look to the right.

With more joints available, the movement was more balanced, used less muscular force, and there was more flow. You changed how you thought about the movement, and you experienced the change by noticing that it felt easier.

Birthday Candle Effect

I refer to the neck as having the "birthday candle effect," because the neck doesn't simply sit on top of the shoulders. A birthday candle doesn't merely sit on top of the icing; it is stuck into the cake and reaches below the surface. The muscles of the neck also reach deeper than what we see at a glance.

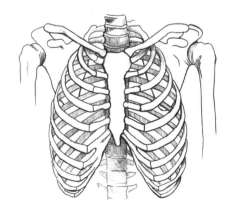

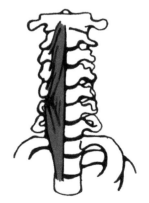

When you move the candle (the neck), all of it moves, not just the visible part. Because the part of the neck below the "surface" is also moving, there is a corresponding movement in the upper torso as well.

Dynamic Relationship: Head and Vertebral Column

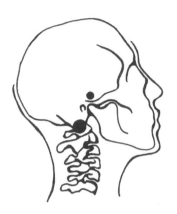

In the illustration on the left, notice the center of gravity of the head, represented by the small solid black disc near the center of the head, and the fulcrum (the head and neck joint), represented by the larger solid black disc.

Notice that the fulcrum and the center of gravity are not at the same point. This fact creates a dynamic relationship.

Because the center of gravity is in front of the fulcrum, the head would fall forward if you did not intend it to be upright. Your intention to be upright is what keeps the head in alignment. The head does not need to be "held."

If you fall asleep while sitting, your head falls forward, and then you catch yourself as you awaken. This happens because of the dynamic relationship between the fulcrum and the center of gravity. Your intention to keep your head upright fades away as you fall asleep and returns only when you jerk awake.

Head and Spine Connection

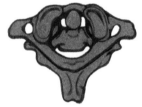

The bone-to-bone connection between the head and the spine is really two joints. The bones that make up these joints are shown from above in this illustration.

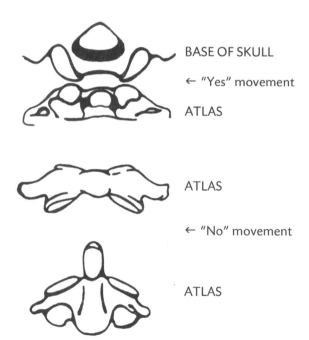

BASE OF SKULL

← "Yes" movement

ATLAS

ATLAS

← "No" movement

ATLAS

The joint between the head and the first vertebra (the atlas) is where the "yes" motion for nodding your head up and down originates.

The joint between the first and second vertebrae (the axis) is where the pivoting motion for turning your head to indicate "no" originates.

These joints are shown in the illustration on the left. The drawing of the skull shows the atlas and axis at the top of the spine. The other drawings show how the atlas and axis fit together to create the "yes" and "no" movements.

On each side of each cervical vertebra is a bony projection called the transverse process. The transverse processes on your first cervical vertebra are larger than those on the other cervical vertebrae. This makes it easier to turn your head.

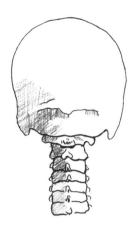

If you put your index fingers on your neck just below your ears and behind your jaw and push lightly, you may be able to feel a bump on each side. You are feeling the first cervical vertebra's transverse processes (the bony projection on each side of each cervical vertebra). This is as close as you can get to a bony reference point for the "top joint."

Cervical Vertebrae

In addition to the atlas (vertebra 1) and the axis (vertebra 2), there are five more cervical vertebrae that make up the neck, as shown in this illustration. (The back of the neck is on the left side of this drawing.)

Spiral Movement of the Neck

When you turn your head, the vertebrae of the neck are designed to bow slightly in the opposite direction (allowing opposition). The overall effect is similar to a spiral staircase. Allowing the neck to bow this way can make a significant impact on the range of movement in your upper back and shoulders.

You can see the spiral in the neck in this study based on Da Vinci's drawing of the Head of Leda.

In contrast to the actual spiral design of the neck, a common misconception is to imagine it like a lollipop, with the head as the candy and the neck as the straight stick.

This false assumption of a straight neck can cause you to hold your neck rigid rather than allowing the counterbalancing spiral motion.

When people allow their necks to spiral, most are also able to feel corresponding movement in their upper backs and sometimes all the way through the back, as shown in this illustration.

Summary

The head is dynamically balanced over the body at the top of the spinal column. The intricate design of the neck allows complex movements as it supports the head. As with other body parts, allowing flexible movement in the neck expands the range of motion in the rest of the body.

Chapter 13

The Arm

If one's elbows or wrists are tense, he is practically nailed down and that's the end of his creative powers.

—CONSTANTIN STANISLAVSKI, IN STANISLAVSKI AND PAVEL RUMYANTSEV, *Stanislavski on Opera*

The structure of the arm includes the shoulder, elbow, wrist, hand, and fingers.

The Quick Version

There is a great deal that can be said about the arm structure. But it can be summarized this way: *The fingertips lead, and everything else follows your intention.*

Keep this thought in mind as we consider key points about the arm.

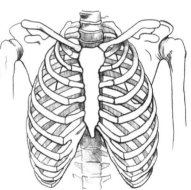

Arm vs. Arm Structure

Most people's conception of their arms extends from the fingertip to the shoulder joint. This is where the seam on your T-shirt is, and it seems to be where your arm joins the rest of the body.

If you extend your arms in front of you, you think of the arms as being what you see. You don't consider that there is more to the arm structure.

If your definition of your arm stops at the shoulder, the chances are very good that when you move your arm, the movement of your shoulder blade will be very limited.

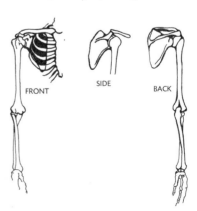

FRONT   SIDE   BACK

There is a joint at the shoulder where the head of the upper arm bone, the humerus, fits against a socket in the scapula.

The broader definition of the arm as an *arm structure* would include the shoulder girdle as well.

Your arm structure is comprised of the collarbone (clavicle), the shoulder blade (scapula), the bones of the arm and hand, and associated muscles.

This illustration shows the rib cage with the scapulae and clavicles highlighted. (The view is from above, of someone facing the bottom of the page.)

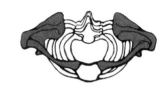

The arm structure rests on top of the ribs, like the milkmaid's yoke in this drawing.

However, since the right scapula (shown below, from the back in the drawing at left and from the side in the drawing at right) is not attached to bones of the torso (the ribs), we can say that there is no bone-to-bone connection of the arm with the torso at the shoulder. The shoulder is a completely free-floating joint.

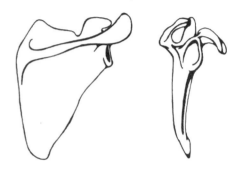

Shoulder Blade Movement

When you move your arm, the shoulder blade must be available to move with your intention. This illustration shows the position of the shoulder blades behind the rib cage when your arms are simply hanging at your sides.

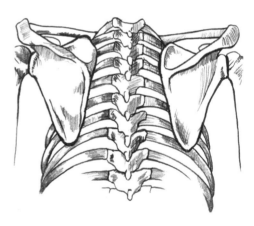

There is a general misconception that shoulder blades are fixed or only move sideways across your back. In reality, shoulder blades move around the torso, up and down, and tilt from side to side, as shown by the multiple figures in this illustration.

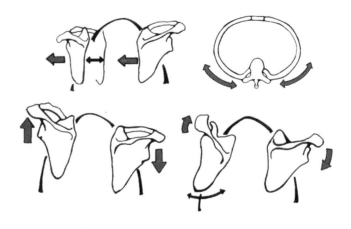

Since the upper arm connects to the scapula at the shoulder joint but the scapula does not connect to the bones of the torso, where exactly does the arm structure connect to the torso?

At the juncture of the collar bone with the sternum or breast plate is a universal joint, . . . it being the only bony union of arm and shoulder with the trunk.
                    —GEORGE B. BRIDGMAN, *Constructive Anatomy*

The shoulder connects to the clavicle, which in turn connects to the sternum. So the bone-to-bone connection between the arm structure and the rib cage is in the center of the chest, where the clavicle and sternum meet at the sternoclavicular joint, as shown in these illustrations (seen from the front). In the shaded drawing, the right clavicle and the top of the sternum are highlighted.

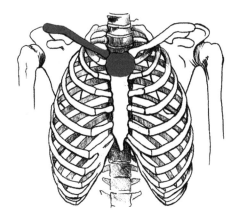 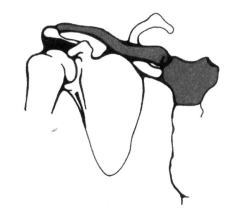

THE COLLARBONE AS SPACER

In addition to connecting the arm structure to the torso at the sternoclavicular joint, the collarbone also works as a spacer (maintaining a specific distance) when you move your arm across your body. However, the general tendency is to lift and pull the shoulder toward the center of the body, compressing the shoulder in the direction that your arm moves as you reach across your body.

This illustration shows the collarbone and shoulder blade movement viewed from above, with the body facing the bottom of the page.

Keep in mind that as your arm moves across your body toward the centerline, the shoulder blade moves in opposition, away from the centerline and around your rib cage.

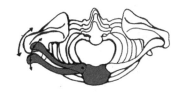

"Position" of the Shoulders

When someone says, "Pull your shoulders back," they mean well; but the idea makes no sense, because, as I've noted, your shoulders are simply resting on top of the upper torso. The "position" of your shoulders is dependent on the underlying structure of the torso.

Holding your shoulders in the "right position" doesn't really work, because when you move, your shoulders have to move, too. The following awareness study illustrates this idea.

AWARENESS STUDY: Shoulders in the "Proper Position"

1. Sit up straight.
2. Put your shoulders in the "proper position."
3. Without moving the shoulders, try to move your arm.
4. Notice that it is not possible to have any range of movement in the arm if the shoulders are held rigid.
5. Now, don't hold your shoulders. As you move your arm, let the shoulders and shoulder blades move. Problem solved.

Muscles That Move the Arm

As I have already described, muscles that move your arm cover almost the entire back, from your sacrum all the way up to the base of the skull. On the front of the body, muscles that move your arm reach below the nipple line and attach at the sternum and the upper humerus and the side of the neck.

You have a flat sheet of muscle on both the front and back of your body. Between these two sheets of muscle is your armpit. When you put your deodorant on in the morning, you are actually putting it over your ribs and between these two sheets of muscle.

Range of Arm Movement

When moving their arms, my students usually start out by moving as if their shoulders are attached to their ribs, as shown in the illustration on the left. This idea doesn't allow the shoulder blade to move, so it limits their range of motion.

After I explain that the collarbone functions as a spacer and that the entire shoulder girdle moves with the arm, my students can usually raise their arms an extra two to four inches, depending on the person. This movement is shown in the illustration on the right.

When a person squeezes the shoulder to move the arm, there is a problem of not allowing opposition. This simple movement problem is a big dilemma for many performing artists—from conductors to flutists to players of string instruments, not to mention actors and dancers.

The solution is quite simple as well. Again, let the collarbone act as a spacer, and allow the shoulder blade to move. Of course, when you are trying to break a habitual movement pattern, this may be easier said than done.

Why Opposition Doesn't Happen When Moving the Arm

When you move your arm, you aren't thinking about opposition. You are so caught up in getting your arm "over there" that your limited focus can cause you to tighten the elbow and the shoulder.

Once you've tightened your muscles and joints, you attempt to move everything in the single direction of your focus. This limited focus excludes the possibility of opposition and counterbalance.

I once coached an elderly woman who hadn't been able to comb her hair in years. As soon as she understood that her shoulder blade needed to move, she was able to touch the top of her head. All she had to do was let her shoulder blade move.

Such coaching only works, of course, if there is no structural damage where we are dealing with a movement pattern problem. But isn't it interesting how our minds can limit how we move?

Elbow Compression

People not only tighten the shoulder when they want to move their arms; almost everyone also tightens the elbow. But almost no one knows that they are doing it. Fortunately, as soon as I point out this tightening/compression to them, most people are able to notice it.

This compression of the elbow is a huge problem, because it really messes up the flow of the arm and body. In my experience, not only do the elbow and shoulder tighten, but the shoulder blade stops moving or is limited, and most people also squeeze their ribs and/or hold their breath. The body becomes static.

It is important for you to know that if anything tightens when you move your arm, that tightening is unnecessary. The flow of your arm movement and your capacity for physical expression will be affected.

I call this restricted movement and compression "leading with the elbow," because it is as if the person is trying to control his or her arm movements from the elbow joint.

It is very easy to see when a person is "leading with the elbow." Shake hands with a friend and watch his or her elbow. If this person is leading with the elbow, the elbow will lift out to the side, as shown on the left in the following illustration.

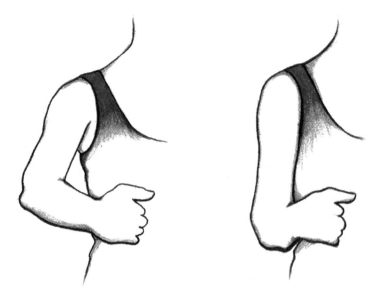

The Elbow Joint

The general perception of the elbow would lead us to believe that it is one simple joint. However, since two different lower arm bones (the radius and the ulna) connect to the upper arm (humerus) at the elbow, it is really a complex joint.

In the following illustration, the right elbow is seen from the back in the drawing on the left. The views on the right show the elbow from the sides.

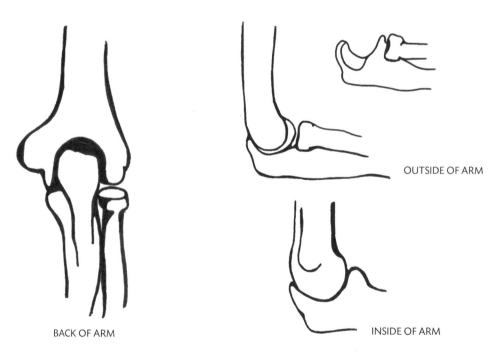

BACK OF ARM

OUTSIDE OF ARM

INSIDE OF ARM

The Forearm

The forearm, from the elbow to wrist, is comprised of the radius and ulna.

The ulna is principally concerned with the bending of the forearm toward or away from the upper arm. The radius is primarily involved with the rotation of the hand.

This illustration shows the right forearm from the front when the hand is held palm up, with the radius on the left.

The Ulna

To help form the elbow joint, the ulna connects to the humerus, in a way that is different than what you might think and that affects how you perceive the arm movement of "bending at the elbow."

Where your forearm attaches to your humerus (upper arm) at the upper end of the ulna, there is a hook-shaped protrusion (the olecranon) into which the lower end of the humerus fits. In this illustration, the olecranon is the large bone at the bottom of the drawing.

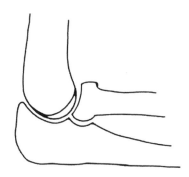

When you lift your hand toward your shoulder, you probably think of the direction of movement as illustrated in this drawing of the right arm (viewed from the back).

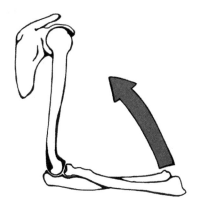

But this way of conceptualizing the movement (bringing the hand to the shoulder) doesn't allow opposition.

In reality, the ulna's hook plays an important part in movement of the arm: by moving the arm as shown below, the olecranon (the hook-shaped projection at the back of the elbow) allows for opposition. When your hand moves toward your shoulder, the hook moves away, making the movement dynamic.

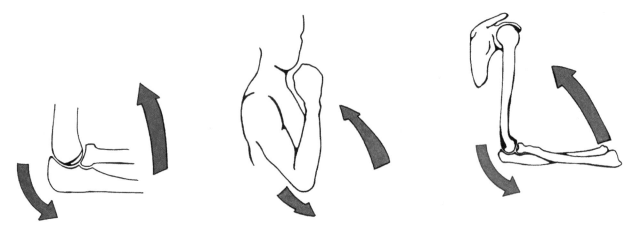

Allowing for opposition in your thinking may help you keep from tightening the elbow when you move your arm.

The Radius

The radius (the lower arm bone on the "thumb side") joins with the ulna (the lower arm bone on the "pinky side") at the base of the humerus to form the elbow joint.

The joint where the radius meets the humerus is similar to a small cup (on the top end of the radius) and ball (at the base of the humerus) as shown in the following illustration.

This design allows the radius to rotate at the elbow as the hand is turned from palm up to palm down and back.

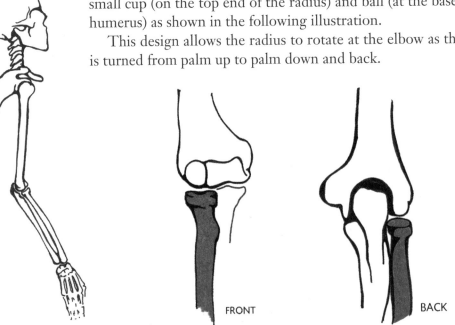

FRONT

BACK

Rotating the Hand

The positional relationship of the radius to the ulna changes when the hand is rotated. (For the arms shown in these illustrations, imagine the elbow at the top of the drawings and the hand at the bottom.)

To begin with, when your right hand is held in front of you, parallel to the floor and palm up, the radius (shaded in these illustrations) and ulna are parallel to each other, as shown in the illustration on the left.

Movement to this position is called *supination*.

When you turn your right hand over so that it is palm down, the radius crosses over the ulna, as shown to the right.

Movement to this position is called *pronation*.

Slightly Different Types of Pronation

According to Blandine Calais-Germain in her book *Anatomy of Movement*, "There are two slightly different types of pronation. In the first (e.g., turning a key), the axis for movement of the hand passes through the middle finger, and the ulna moves slightly [*i.e., the ulna is not held rigid and moves slightly laterally*] in conjunction with the radius . . . In the second (e.g., flipping the page of a book), the axis of the hand passes through the fifth finger, and the ulna remains fixed." For clarification, the ulna does not rotate in either movement, but it does not need to be held rigid either.

"Getting" this idea is very important for instrumentalists, conductors, and actors.

These two movements are illustrated below, with pronation around the different axes.

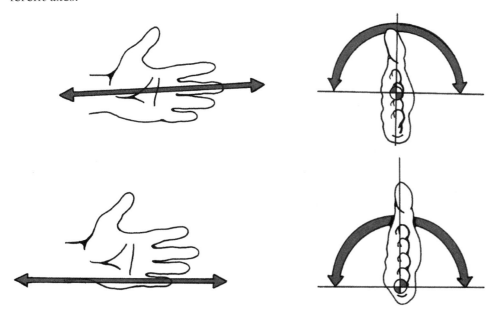

When you want to break a habit of compression while turning the hand, it is helpful to

1. initially use the pinky as your frame of reference for the axis of rotation;
2. simply know that for a lot of movements, the axis is probably somewhere in between the pinky and the middle finger.

Avoid holding the elbow still when moving the hand. It doesn't need to move, but it also doesn't need to be held still.

Another Look at Rotating the Hand

When you rotate your hand, it may be helpful if you think of the movement as not originating in the hand at all. It is really the radius that is rotating. Since the muscles that actually do the rotating are in the forearm, that is where the movement happens.

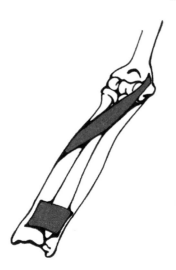

Instead of focusing on moving the hand, students who substitute an awareness that the hand is moving from the forearm usually find the movement much easier to make.

This illustration shows the right forearm, viewed from the front, with the arm held as it would look if you were seeing the palm of the right hand.

Technically, this is what happens: although the pronator teres (in this drawing, the shaded muscle located near the elbow) is the major pronator of the forearm (i.e., the major muscle that rotates the forearm so that the hand faces downward or backward), it works with the pronator quadratus (in this drawing, the shaded muscle located near the wrist). The brachioradialis (not pictured) can assist in the initial stages of supination/pronation.

Wrists, Hands, and Fingers Simplified

An understanding of wrists, hands, and fingers is very complicated. For our purposes, the movements of the hands and fingers can be simplified to two basic concepts: oppositional movements and expansive movements.

All of the following hand movements are based on just one idea involving these two concepts. If you allow oppositional movement to occur when you move your hand, the movement will be more expansive, and there will be less compression in the wrist.

Let's look at some examples of what it means to allow oppositional and expansive movement.

Compression at the Wrist

Normally, when you lift your hand off a table top, this movement of the hand is conceptualized as bringing the back of the hand toward you, as shown in this illustration.

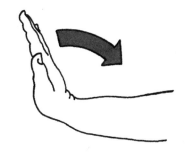

However, think about what happens when you allow opposition and expansion, a concept that I've repeated over and over again (with descriptions of the foot, elbow, hip, head and neck, etc.).

Opposition When Moving the Hand

When you allow opposition while moving the hand, the heel of the hand moves away from you as the fingers come toward you, as shown on the right.

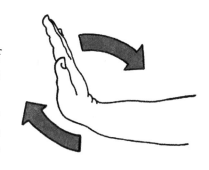

This creates expansion, and you will feel lengthening at the bottom of the wrist. However, that doesn't mean that the top of the wrist has to compress. Compression in the wrist would happen only if the heel didn't move away.

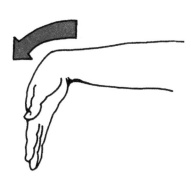

If you move your hand in the opposite direction (i.e., if you extend the hand downward as shown to the left), the opposition happens in the opposite direction. In other words, as the top of the hand moves away from you, the heel of your hand moves toward you (opposition).

You don't have to compress the bottom of the wrist (i.e., it doesn't have to tighten) to make this movement. Instead, the top of the wrist lengthens, and the bottom of the wrist expands.

Moving the Hand Sideways

Moving the hand in a sideways motion is similar in concept to the previous up-and-down hand movement.

The tendency is to compress in the direction you move the hand.

Instead, as you move the hand laterally (to the side) left or right, feel the wrist lengthen (the oppositional movement), and allow the opposite side of the wrist to expand as well.

Fingers and Opposition

A simple way of using this opposition/expansion approach for moving the hands and fingers is to think of the hand gripping a ball, as shown here. Imagine the hand expanding around the ball instead of squeezing it. In other words, your fingers are moving away from the wrist instead of compressing toward it.

The principal anatomical reference for this movement is the fact, noted in chapter 6, that the third joint of each finger is actually in the hand and not at the crease where the finger joins the hand.

Summary

A simple way of thinking about moving the arm and hand is to acknowledge that your whole body follows your intention.

In a particular instance (e.g., grasping a latte), it is your hand that is closest to your intention.

Think of moving with all the muscles and joints available. The muscles don't bind the joints. As you allow opposition, the arm expands into movement.

When you move your arm, let your fingertips lead, and allow everything else to follow your intention.

Chapter 14
Summarizing Anatomy

The inherent design of your body is dynamic and not static. Everything we've learned about anatomy can be summarized in a few basic concepts. Let's review them.

The Dynamic Body and Expression

Remember the dynamic model of the body that we constructed earlier. You now have a clearer picture of how the muscles relate to the skeleton. You can see how the body must move in patterns rather than parts. Think how daunting the task would be if we actually had to control this dynamic design consciously.

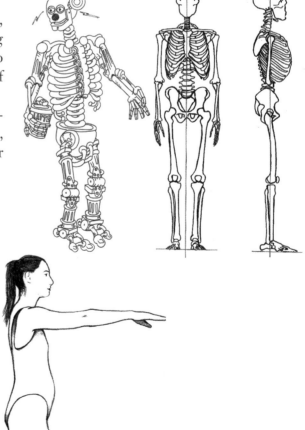

In the past, when we tried to correct our posture, the process usually involved holding something still. All we were doing was throwing a chink into the pattern, keeping that part out of the pattern of flow.

Not only when you perform in your art, movement, or sports activity but in everyday life as well, the more of you that you allow to move, the greater your capacity for expression will be.

Putting It All Together: A Practical Application

Now that we have expanded your understanding of the body's anatomy, let's put your new information into action and allow it to inform another awareness study.

To do so, let's go back to one of the very first movements we used when we discussed balance, force, and flow: arms raised in front of the body and held parallel to the floor, as shown in this illustration.

We used this movement to illustrate the differences between dynamic balance and static imbalance. Now let's back it up with some anatomy.

AWARENESS STUDY: More Is Moving

1. Put yourself in the configuration in the illustration on the bottom of page 151: extend just your right arm forward and parallel to the ground.

When you put yourself in this position, it is still possible to maintain static imbalance and move just one arm.

2. Next, extend your left arm forward so that both arms are parallel to the floor in front of you.

It is even more work now to maintain this static imbalance, but it is still possible to move your arms more or less just from your shoulder joint.

3. Now rotate your left arm so that it is at shoulder level but extended in the opposite direction (behind you instead of in front). Your left arm is now like your right arm, only behind your body.

Experience the counterbalancing and flow of the movement (i.e., how your torso moves to accommodate this movement).

4. Do this movement again, and this time try not to let your torso move.

Do you see how hard it is to stop your torso from counterbalancing now that you understand what counterbalancing is?

With your new awareness, you now experience more of your body moving.

Now that you've studied how the body moves with balance, force, and flow, and now that you have a better understanding of your anatomy, it may be easier for you to appreciate that expressive movement requires dynamic balance.

Anatomy Impacts Movement

We have learned so many things about our anatomy that have an impact on movement. Understanding the body's anatomy enables you to find greater expression in your movement in everyday life and while performing. It makes your movement more expansive and expressive.

For example, think of our redefinition of arm structure, as shown in these illustrations.

Consider all the shaded muscles that move and are part of the overall movement pattern called "moving your arm." Add this concept of the redefined arm (and other body parts) to the ideas of opposition and counterbalance, and you now allow your movements to be more inclusive.

Another concept that impacts your movement is the fact that your spine is contracting and expanding with the movement. Plus you are breathing.

In the illustration below are two views of the skeleton, one superimposed on the other.

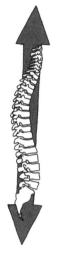

The background skeleton is centered around the centerline (line of balance).

The shaded view illustrates another concept: the compensatory pattern that we've learned most people exhibit.

Now we are right back to implied limitations, as illustrated here.

To get to this point, our discussion has had to be a linear progression. But in point of fact, the act of performing is anything but linear. We have taken a linear progression through the inclusive and simultaneous.

Summary

The head and neck, the lungs and rib cage, the pelvic bowl and abdominal cavity, the body's core, and the arms and legs and feet and hands all work and balance together. I call this interrelationship "suspension."

Even though I discuss "parts"—such as the head, arms, or feet—in these chapters, I have demonstrated that this distinction is for conceptual convenience only. The entire body moves together.

In the final analysis, we arrive at a very different concept of the body from where we started. Rather than having a static body that is held still in order to move in parts in sequential fashion, we now have a vision of a dynamic body—moving in patterns—in which muscles overlap, interrelate, and are simultaneous in movement.

Keeping the entire body available while you gesture increases your capacity for physical expression.

For every muscle pulling in one direction, there must be the corresponding muscle pulling in the opposite direction. Muscles are therefore paired . . . [F]or every flexor on the front there must be its corresponding extensor on the back.

—GEORGE B. BRIDGMAN, *Constructive Anatomy*

Part Four

In the Moment

Nothing happens until something moves. —ALBERT EINSTEIN

Chapter 15
Awareness—The Key to Availability

Stanislavski did not recognize any beauty in gesture or pose for its own sake; he always insisted on some action behind it.

—PAVEL RUMYANTSEV, IN CONSTANTIN STANISLAVSKI
AND RUMYANTSEV, *Stanislavski on Opera*

As a performer, you will find that being aware of your tension patterns and being available for movement will enable you to be "in the moment" and will free your capacity for expression.

Performing

You have dedicated your life to your medium of choice—music, art, theater, the dance, or whatever activity you choose to do with artistic expression.

You desire to connect with the people around you, to speak to your audience from the platform that is the stage, to share with them your brief glimpse of life and your insight into what it means to be alive.

Your ideas, thoughts, insights, vision, understanding, perceptions, and feelings span the abyss of the dark theater or concert hall and touch another's life. You carry the hope that in some small way, perhaps ever so slightly, you can make a difference. That your gift might affect another, who in turn might affect another, perhaps even nudging the course of human existence toward a more humane and inclusive direction.

Performing is your raison d'être. This is a noble ambition. It requires much personal and financial sacrifice as well.

In everyday life, "if" is a fiction; in the theatre "if" is an experiment. In everyday life, "if" is an evasion; in the theatre "if" is the truth. When we are persuaded to believe in this truth then the theatre and life are one. This is a high aim. It sounds like hard work. To play needs much work. But when we experience the work as play, then it is not work any more. A play is play.

—PETER BROOK, *The Empty Space*

Developing Awareness

In our efforts to increase our capacity for expression, we need to assimilate the idea of moving from expansion rather than from compression. I call this way of moving *availability*. Your joints and muscles are available to flow with your intention. But before you can be available, you need to develop an awareness of your habitual patterns.

Awareness is the key to availability. So let's discuss the process of developing awareness and the ways we can expand our awareness when we perform.

The Process

When you learn a new physical skill—and it really doesn't matter what skill we're talking about—you are usually given a lot of instructions and things to *do*.

With movement and expression, the process is different. You have a lot of things to *undo*, so that you can restore the natural design. You improve your efficiency not by doing *more* but by doing *less*. In other words, your old movement habits require a lot of excess effort (doing more), but as you allow your movement to flow with balance and appropriate force (doing less), you move more efficiently.

Changing movement patterns is the process of noticing and allowing.

If you don't know what you are doing, you have no choice: you are stuck with a habit that blocks movement. Awareness is an important step in itself, because when you have awareness, you have the opportunity to interrupt your old ways of moving.

The Progression

Using what you've learned in this book, you can now notice your habit of stopping movement. Because you have this greater awareness, you can simply reduce the effort and allow the additional movement to flow through your body. In doing so, you are allowing your body to counterbalance, and you will be able to feel yourself come into balance.

You feel movement. You also feel lack of movement, evidenced by compression, stillness, tension, limited movement, stopping, holding, tightening, and holding your breath. Sometimes you are actually holding your breath; sometimes you are metaphorically holding your body's breath. Now, when you notice any lack of movement, you will allow movement throughout your body.

THE LONG-TERM CHANGE

Each time you go through the progression of *noticing* and *allowing*, you increase the percentage of movement and the overall efficiency of your body. After you go through this progression, your body will retain some of the additional capacity you've gained. You won't go all the way back to square one.

Then, the next time you become aware that you are blocking movement, it will be a little less of a block. Little by little, over time and with patience and practice, your habits change, and how you move becomes more efficient. As your efficiency increases, so does the percentage of your body that is moving. As this percentage climbs, so does the effectiveness of your physical expression.

Awareness of Your Range of Motion

As you become more aware of your body and the way you habitually move, it's easy to fall into judging yourself, looking at your movement as good or bad. This makes change harder. I like to think about positive change as a simple matter of increasing efficiency. It takes away the "good" and "bad" labels.

When my son was about two years old, I would peek in on him while he was sleeping. Occasionally his torso would be fully arched backward. I asked myself, "When, in going about our daily business, do we ever explore that range of motion?"

For example, we sit and slump, and we know the slump is bad. It is natural to want to correct the slump, so we try to sit up straight. The range of motion we are exploring goes from forward to vertical. But what about the range of motion that is behind vertical? If we are going to be "wrong" on the front side, shouldn't we explore being "wrong" on the back side as well? It seems a more balanced approach to be "wrong" both ways and then find the middle ground.

If I was my torso, I think that it would be a lot easier for me to find the middle ground if I explored the full range of motion.

This is why it's important to include activities like stretching or yoga in your life. Doing so keeps your physical instrument tuned.

AWARENESS STUDY: Range of Motion

For this study, "be" your body.

1. Go from forward slump to vertical.
2. Then go from vertical to arched back (backward slump), and explore the full range of motion (you will feel the front of your body expand).

To me, this seems to be a much easier way to find balance than to merely look for the "fix."

When you explore your full range of motion, the muscles that had to tighten and stop moving as you held yourself forward in a slump now have to move. When you go backward beyond vertical, you are no longer looking for balance with muscles still configured around a slump.

It's easier to find balance if you first break the pattern of compensation. Exploring your full range of motion breaks up old patterns, opens more options, and makes it easier for you to allow movement.

When you are playing/performing, how much of yourself and your surroundings are you really aware of?

Let's use playing the flute as an example. You be the flute player. We'll call the various areas of awareness surrounding you "circles of attention."

I think it is safe to say that the first circle of attention (where your initial awareness goes) includes the flute, your mouth, your face, and maybe your hands.

The second circle of attention includes the upper body (from the waist up) and perhaps your breathing. (I often watch flute players perform in a workshop setting. It would probably be safe to say that the second circle includes only the front of the upper body).

The third circle of attention extends to the music stand and music. Let me remind you that your eyes don't radiate your vision out to the score like a beam from a lighthouse. The eyes allow the image in; the music comes to you. That's what allows you to include the back of your upper body in this circle of awareness.

The fourth circle of attention includes an awareness of your entire body.

The fifth circle includes any fellow performers.

The sixth circle includes the audience.

There could be more subdivisions for the circles of attention: these circles are arbitrary. Expanding your awareness is the point of this discussion of circles. When you perform, as you include more circles of attention and open your awareness, you will find it easier to remain supple and expressive.

Availability—Allowing Movement

Now let's consider how being available allows your joints and muscles to move with your intention, which allows you to move with greater expression.

> There is no one single muscle that controls one single motion; all the compartments must work in concert to produce graceful and efficient movement.
>
> —DEANE JUHAN, *Job's Body*

What happens when you notice that you are limiting your movement, metaphorically holding your breath? This is a no-brainer: you want to stop holding your breath and start to breathe; that is, you want to allow movement.

"Allow" Defined

As I've already noted, the progression of awareness requires that you first notice and then allow. You allow the movement to happen. But what does it mean to "allow"? And where do you go after you allow?

Allowing is having the muscles available to move. Allowing is being in dynamic balance.

Releasing and Letting Go

The language that we use as we conceptualize movement is very powerful. The term *allow* is different from the terms *let it go* or *release it*. With *let it go* or *release it*, the focus is on the "it," the tension; the focus is on you, not on what you're doing. With *allow*, you are making it possible for your body to be available to your intention (performing). You are including and not excluding.

The ability to let go is important, but it is not the final goal. Once you let go of the tension that results from compensations, the goal is to stay available for movement.

WHEN YOU ARE ABLE TO RELEASE

There is a catch-22 or recurring pattern that people can find themselves in once they are able to notice that they are holding. First, they become aware of the holding and let go. When they let go, they fall all the way into a collapse, which, in turn, causes them to hold again. They fall out of holding in one direction and fall into holding in the other direction. Eventually they notice that they are holding again. Then, because they are now collapsed as well, they find themselves tightening to move again. It's an insidious cycle of tightening and flopping.

Remember, if you take the pressure off a spring, it goes up (and down); it doesn't flop. To get yourself out of this loop of tensing and releasing, think of letting go as *allowing movement*.

Gaining Awareness

In a sense, as you begin the process of changing how you move, you need to consider everything that we've discussed, because everything (aesthetics, language, assumptions, implied limitations, how you focus, your vision, thoughts about movement, myths, your understanding of your anatomy, your sense of effort, including/excluding, etc.) affects how you move, and everything has some part to play in every movement that you make. Everything influences everything.

Since it is impossible to constantly keep in mind everything and its effect on everything else, you can simplify the task by using as your guide the simple dictum "Everything is moving."

To help my students gain the awareness that everything is moving, I normally introduce awareness tools in a class or workshop setting. Knowing that they have worked for my students, I present these awareness tools to you in this chapter. Don't expect them all to work for you. If you can find a few that are meaningful or speak to you, that's great! Then we have introduced some approaches that have helped you increase your awareness.

My hope is to pique your interest, give you a glimpse of what might be possible, and provide you with a few ways to get started.

The Formula for Change

Use the following simple formula for change while you explore the awareness tools in this chapter: *While . . . in relation to . . . allow.*

This formula describes a process that is simultaneous and synchronous with what you are doing. It is not something you do consciously. It works like this:

While I lift my arm, I notice what is going on with my arm. Let's say that while I am lifting my arm, I notice that my elbow is still or tight.

In relation to the holding pattern in my arm, I look for compensations in the rest of my body. These compensations are a result of what is not moving in my arm.

I *allow* movement in the rest of my body. Rather than concentrate on fixing my arm and putting my focus on my arm (which would be an excluding focus), I take the opposite approach and include the rest of my body. I allow movement of the compensations that are made in the rest of my body in relation to the arm's stillness.

When the compensations are no longer present in the rest of my body, the tension in my arm softens.

This formula can be used with all the awareness tools.

The Awareness Tools

The following awareness tools are designed to help you notice when you are holding your breath, figuratively and literally in your torso, while you perform. In fact, as we will see, holding your breath can, in itself, be an awareness tool.

The first couple of awareness tools are an easy way to start. You can use them almost any time and anywhere and can apply them to any activity.

AWARENESS TOOL: *Soft Surface/Feet Soft*

No matter what you are doing (right now as you read this book, when you are walking, when you buy a latte), notice if the surface of your body is soft. If it isn't soft, allow it to soften. Suppose you are going to conduct or to do a monologue. Think, "Am I soft?" Suppose you are doing a yoga asana (posture). It is my observation that most people tighten in order to stretch. Instead, you might think, "Am I soft?"

In the same way, your feet should remain soft—not tensed.

There's no need to stop what you're doing to check whether you are soft or not. Just continue and let yourself be soft. Include softness.

If you can let the surface of your body and your feet be a little softer as you go about your business, you have just made a huge impact on your ability to perform.

Your practice session is the time to pay attention to stillness and to soften while you're rehearsing. When you perform, forget about it.

Performance is your time to live in the moment. If you are in the moment, it is impossible to be thinking about what is or is not moving, and you don't want to be thinking about that anyway. What you are doing is what you are doing. You aren't judging. You are performing, living. This is the payoff.

After all, who wants to be thinking about movement when you have a chance to create magic that can touch your fellow human beings? This is the real reason you are reading this book in the first place.

Eventually, as you become a more skilled artist, such things as opening your focus and including a physical awareness while you experience the moment will become second nature. You will sense a total physical availability as you perform. You will not be holding yourself. You will be free to resonate with the moment. Your availability and your intention will be one. This is where the path to awareness is taking you.

AWARENESS TOOL: *Everyday Awareness*

It's the little things of everyday life that present you with a moment of opportunity. If awareness isn't part of your life on a day-to-day basis, it surely isn't going to be there under the stress of performance.

So, as you pick up your coat, put your arm in the sleeve, and put the coat on, ask yourself, "Do I really have to hold myself still? Do I really need to hold my breath just to button my coat?" If you happen to notice that the surface of your body is still while you are buttoning, just include more movement. Don't stop yourself and say, "Oh, I was wrong." No judging.

AWARENESS TOOL: *Support the Gesture*

When you make a gesture, having someone or something support the weight of your movement will allow you to become aware of any holding and compensations. You can then allow movement freely, becoming more expressive in the process.

Here is an example of how I use this awareness tool when I work with conductors.

First, I ask them to lift the baton in preparation for conducting. As soon as I ask them to lift the baton, that's the only thing they can think about. Of course, their focus goes to their arms, and the rest of the body tightens, because they aren't thinking about including it.

I could have said, "Move your body in such a way that the baton goes up." That would have been a more inclusive way to state my request.

The second thing I do is reach out to each conductor and support the weight of his or her arms. Immediately, the conductor becomes aware of unnecessary tension and the compensations that are being made to offset that weight shift. Finally, this awareness leads to movement.

APPLYING THE FORMULA FOR CHANGE

Here's how the formula for change can be applied to the awareness tool called "Support the Gesture."

While their batons are raised and still, I ask the conductors to notice the compensations in their bodies *in relation to* the act of raising their arms.

Then, I support the arms and suggest that the conductors *allow* movement to replace the compensations.

Once I support the weight of the arms, there is no need for the conductors to compensate. All at once, where there was stillness, there is now movement. It is absolutely delightful to see movement flood through the body and to watch the conductors become more expressive and lively.

AWARENESS TOOL: *Support the Gesture with Partner*

A two-person version of the awareness tool called "Support the Gesture" is a great exercise to get started with. It is performed with a partner. It is such a simple concept, but it really works.

AWARENESS STUDY: A Partner Supports the Arm

1. Bring your right arm up in front of you, parallel with the floor, as the model in the illustration to the left is doing. (Remember, you can apply this awareness tool to any gesture or movement.)
2. As shown in the next illustration, have your partner support your arm so that you can let the arm completely relax.

In this exercise, you give your partner the weight of your arm. The moment you let the arm relax, there is movement in the rest of your body.

The idea behind this awareness study is to reveal how you have been compensating in other parts of the body. (Most students feel movement in their shoulders and lower back and maybe even in their hips, knees, and feet.)

When the arm relaxes, the places where you feel movement are the areas where you have been compensating (habitually holding/tensing) when raising your arm.

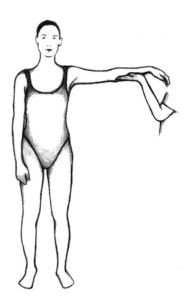

3. Now try the same exercise except lift your arm to the side, as shown in this illustration.
4. Have your partner support your arm.
5. Experience the movement.

HOW IT WORKS

The moment your partner supports your raised arm, the compensation in the torso becomes unnecessary, and movement is allowed. The pattern of compensation is immediately revealed. The next time you make this movement, see if you can raise your arm while allowing a little more movement in the rest of your body.

AWARENESS TOOL: *Support the Gesture with an Inanimate Object*

Using an inanimate object to support your gesture is not only a great tool for making the gesture easier, it also spawns an entire family of awareness activities.

You can do these awareness studies by yourself. Any activity you can do with an object that can support your weight will work. Following are two examples.

AWARENESS STUDY: Hands on a Steering Wheel

When most people grasp a steering wheel, they hold their elbows out to the side unnecessarily, as shown in the drawing on the left below. Here's a way to let the inanimate object (the steering wheel) help you.

1. Put your hands on the steering wheel.
2. Let the steering wheel support the weight of your arms.
3. Relax your arms.
4. Notice that you can let your arms hang or "drape" downward from the steering wheel, as shown in the drawing on the right below.

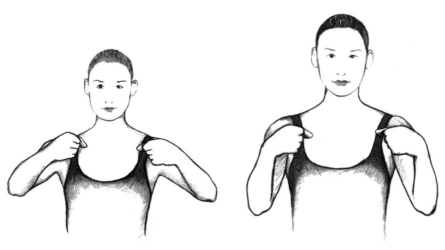

AWARENESS STUDY: Opening a Door

You can use the same "inanimate object" concept when opening a door.

1. Put your hand on a doorknob.
2. Let the doorknob support the weight of the hand and arm as shown here.
3. Relax your arm.
4. Notice that, as with the preceding exercise with the steering wheel, when you relax your hand and arm, the compensations in the arm and in the rest of your body are revealed.

HOW IT WORKS

The preceding exercises work the same way as having a person support a gesture for you. The unnecessary compensation in the torso is revealed, and then you can release the tension and allow movement.

This concept of allowing an object to support your weight can be applied to numerous activities: hands on a desk, hands on a music stand, and so on.

AWARENESS TOOL: *Nonhabitual Choice*

Making a nonhabitual choice is a good way to identify the compensations that would normally accompany a given gesture.

This tool is a really basic one that can be used with almost any gesture. I use the doorknob again in the following awareness study.

AWARENESS STUDY: Opening a Door with the Nondominant Hand

1. Instead of opening a door with your dominant hand, try the other hand (if you're right-handed, use your left hand, or vice versa).
2. Notice that this movement is less tense than when you use your dominant hand.

In the preceding awareness study, just using your nondominant hand is enough to make the compensatory pattern discernible as you gesture. When you reach for the door with your nondominant hand, all at once you are able to notice the tension and lack of movement in your torso. You habitually fire up the pattern to open a door, but when you use your nondominant hand, the habitual pattern no longer works.

AWARENESS TOOL: *Holding Your Breath*

Another exercise that can help you become aware of compensatory patterns involves holding your breath and then moving. As with earlier exercises, you can apply this awareness concept to any activity (tying shoes, putting on a coat, etc.).

AWARENESS STUDY: Holding the Breath While Reaching for a Doorknob

1. While holding your breath, reach for a doorknob.
2. Grasp the doorknob as shown in the illustration.
3. After you grasp the doorknob, exhale.
4. As you reach for the door, notice the tightness caused by holding your breath. Then, as you exhale, you will feel the movement.

I like to use the following awareness study to help students become aware of compression in the head, neck, and upper chest area.

Some students sort this out right away. Others simply don't experience the movement, so don't worry if you aren't able to experience it. If you push your head forward just a bit, it will exaggerate your old habit and make the movement more obvious.

1. Hold your breath and reach as high as you can toward the ceiling with both arms, as shown in the illustration to the right.
2. Then stop holding your breath.
3. Feel the movement in your arms, upper torso, head, and neck, as shown in the illustration on the left.

Many students feel their heads and necks move upward when they stop holding their breath. It is as if someone took the pressure off a spring.

Remember, your spine is contracting and expanding with every breath you take and every move you make.

HOW IT WORKS

Stopping your breath limits movement. When you exhale or inhale after holding your breath, you feel movement. You gain awareness of what was not moving while you weren't breathing.

AWARENESS TOOL: *Moving While You're Moving*

A simple concept that is designed to address the habit of holding yourself still in order to move is to do just the opposite: make more than one movement at the same time. This idea is used in tai chi all the time.

The idea behind asking you to make a gesture while you're moving is to have you experience a new option.

AWARENESS STUDY: Moving While Raising the Arm

Let's start this study by making a single gesture.

1. Allow your weight to balance on your right foot.
2. Raise your left arm out to the side, as shown in this illustration.

Unless you consciously refrained from tensing, this movement originated from stillness; that is, you made yourself still and then raised your arm.

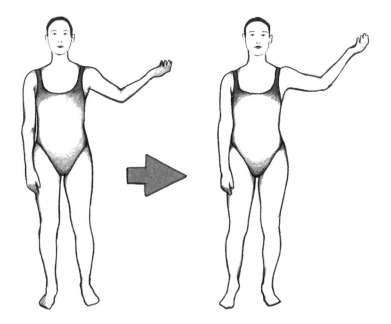

3. Now try shifting your weight from the right leg to the left leg while you raise your arm.

4. Notice how different it feels to move without holding yourself still.

HOW IT WORKS

This is a helpful awareness tool. I don't mean to imply that you should always wiggle your hips from side to side when you move your arms. The reason for shifting the weight from one foot to the other in the preceding exercise is simply to take your focus off the arm movement.

The goal of the exercise is to be available. Allow yourself to experience how different it feels when you make a gesture while moving and without holding yourself still to initiate movement.

In reality, the movement that would naturally occur in the body as you lift your arm is the oppositional movement that would counterbalance the change in weight.

Unfortunately, when we hold ourselves still, we interrupt this natural flow and block the natural movement. When you are "moving while you move," you get a glimpse of what it feels like to move without first holding yourself still. Try this tool the next time you are rehearsing.

AWARENESS TOOL: *Making a Second Gesture*

One of the ways to gain awareness of your compensatory patterns is by making a second gesture and observing what happens. I love this exercise. However, it might take you a couple of attempts to sort it out.

We could use any gesture to illustrate this tool, but I've selected a gesture that I find works well with students who've never tried it before.

1. Raise your left arm toward the ceiling, as shown in the illustration on the right.
2. Now make a second gesture with your right arm. Bringing your right arm up parallel to the floor and reaching behind you (as shown below) usually works.

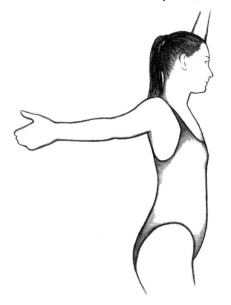

3. As soon as you finish making the second gesture, notice the compression (what I like to call "congestion") in the torso.
4. Allow this area of congestion to move.

While moving the right arm structure, most of my students notice the compensation in the torso.

5. If you don't experience movement right away, expand your focus.

Try not to focus on one or both arms. Instead, keep your focus open, including the entire body.

HOW IT WORKS

When you make the first gesture, it sets up a series of compensations in the rest of the body in relation to this gesture and the subsequent distribution of weight.

When you make the second gesture, the compensations for the first gesture don't work anymore. The weight distribution is different. Since the compensations are no longer needed, it is relatively easy to allow the resultant movement.

As with all the awareness tools that make you aware of compensatory patterns, the point of this tool is to reach a state of availability.

Note that it is important that you move sequentially, making the first gesture and then the second. If you move both arms at the same time, this exercise won't work.

THE STATE OF AVAILABILITY

The following steps are necessary to reach the state of availability.

1. You make a gesture, and there is a compensation as a result of the imbalance.
2. You make a second gesture, and as a result you gain awareness of the compensation.
3. You allow movement, and the compensation disappears.

Instead of just letting the tension go and then settling into a new pattern of holding and compensations, you want to extend this moment of allowing movement in your entire body (availability) while you gesture with your intention. Let the spring go! Let yourself go!

Availability is the capacity for expression.

Final Thoughts

In the final analysis, no one can keep all of these thoughts and concepts in his or her consciousness and expect to get anything accomplished.

What is important is to be *aware* of your intention and of how much of your body is *available* to that intention. To help you include all this information as you follow your intention, simply say, "Everything is moving," as you move.

Standing in the Rain

While at a summer camp for symphony conductors, I was in my cabin one evening trying to find a good way to explain the relationship between performance and the idea that everything is moving. As I sat there, I started to hear raindrops hitting the roof, drop after drop, almost one drop at time. Gradually the shower intensified, and finally it began to pour rain. Then it hit me: you can't count raindrops.

If you try to count each individual raindrop, you are lost. It's impossible. There are too many drops to count. If you count one, you exclude others. Similarly, in a performance, you can't focus on, for example, only the oboe or the violin or yourself. A singular focus excludes.

You can't count raindrops in a rainstorm. You simply have to stand in the rain and let it pour. When you are in the moment, you include; you are aware and available; you experience and resonate with the storm.

Chapter 16

Artist to Artist

I am enough of an artist to draw freely upon my imagination.
Imagination is more important than knowledge. Knowledge
is limited. Imagination circles the world.
—ALBERT EINSTEIN

We're talking artist to artist now. Here, from my performance journal, are a few notes and observations on playing and performing that I would like to share with you. This chapter is not meant to be a formalized discussion but, rather, contains excerpts from conversations with my students, as well as additional thoughts on movement.

Challenges

In trying to make your performance more dynamic, you face two types of challenge.

The Physical Challenge. Physically, the challenge facing you is to discover habituated patterns of movement that you may not even know are there. These undiscovered patterns limit the potential of your practice sessions and performances.

The Mental Challenge. Mentally, the challenge facing you is to discover the myriad ideas and assumptions that influence your moving and performing. You are holding on to some of these constructs. Perhaps you are not quite ready to give them up. Some come from so long ago that you would not even remember where they came from or the reason why you adopted them in the first place. Still others are there at an almost unconscious level.

Meeting the Challenge. In order to span the abyss of human communication (i.e., to reach beyond the footlights to your audience), you develop your physical instrument's capacity for expression so that it is capable of communicating the slightest nuance of a clear and pure intention. Your body and mind are one available instrument, allowing you to live in the integrity of the moment. You experience the act of performing. Your gestures, thoughts, and actions are honest and true.

Formula for Movement. To move with expression, your formula for movement is simply

Intention
Joints available
Body follows weight shifts

All this happens simultaneously while you resonate in the moment of creation. You are ready to begin.

Preparation

Preparation is the key to performance. If you are adequately prepared (lines learned, music practiced, lyrics understood), you are free to experience. You have all your bases covered. If you are trying to remember what is coming (in the music, in the script), that is what you are doing— *remembering*. If you are remembering, you are out of the moment.

Commitment to Being in the Moment

The goal while performing is for you to experience your intention while you are aware of technical considerations. To be "in the moment," your body and mind must be available to the moment.

It is fair to say that not everyone wants to make this commitment. Many look for reasons why this commitment to being in the moment is not the preferable approach for performing. Most of the reasons not to be in the moment are rooted in fear. It is less frightening to sit back and be safe, to rely on the technical aspects of performing without worrying about intention.

Personally, I don't want to see a "safe" performance. We all have witnessed a technically perfect performance and have walked away saying, "So what?"

Performing in the Moment. In truth, it's virtually impossible to be completely "in the moment" for an entire performance. Performing, like moving your body, is a balancing act.

You are on a tightrope. On one side of the tightrope are all of the technical considerations, and on the other side is the act of experiencing your intention. Being in the moment is finding the perfect balance between these two approaches while performing.

What we are after is to spend as much time as possible in the moment. This means that a successful performance is not evaluated in terms of being in the moment or not but by how much of the performance was in the moment. We can think of being in the moment as controlled not by an on/off switch but by a dimmer.

While. A key to performing "in the moment" is using the word *while*. *While* I am aware of the technical considerations, I am also experiencing my intention. Making "while moments" a part of your intention allows you to keep your focus open. It allows you to focus on a specific concern without narrowing your focus and excluding your surroundings. *While I focus on my left hand, I am also aware of my body. While I focus on the soloist, I am also aware of the orchestra.*

The summation of all the "while moments" is the complete performance.

Living in this "while moment" for an hour and a half on stage requires an enormous amount of availability. You are tired at the end of the performance—not because of the physical exertion, but because of the psychic energy you've expended.

Working your way through the performance is like canoeing through white water. If you just let the river take you, you will smash on the rocks. If you don't look ahead, you won't know where the downstream rocks are. So while you are avoiding the rock that is your immediate concern, you are also looking ahead.

You work your way through the white water one obstacle at a time, one paddle stroke at a time. Each stroke is different and appropriate to the needs of the moment. Your strokes need to be sometimes stronger, sometimes lighter, sometimes pulling, other times pushing. The summation of all the individual maneuvers is canoeing the rapids—the performance.

To Be: Being a Vessel

When you perform, your job is to be a vessel that resonates with the music or words that you are performing. This is the first step. In acting, it is referred to as the "to be."

"To be" is the general tone or understanding of the emotional content of the scene. In music, it would be the feeling of the phrase or passage.

For instance, you know what it feels like to reunite with someone you love, especially after a long separation. That general understanding of what this experience feels like is what is meant by the "to be" energy. You know what the scene is supposed to feel like, because you have been there, done that.

The "to be" is not an end unto itself. This is where a lot of performers run amuck. The "to be" is a by-product of the "to do"—of what you are doing/experiencing. The "to do" is what you are doing specifically. The "to be" is the general feeling of the scene.

You can't perform or act a generality. There is nothing to experience. You can experience only the specific moment.

Actors understand the tone of a scene. However, it is not your job to try to manufacture that tone (i.e., to create the "to be").

For example, in real life, you don't manufacture happiness for the sake of making happiness. You don't walk over to someone you love, make yourself happy, and then say, "Hello." The happiness comes about because you see the person, open your arms, embrace, and so on. The "doing" (extending a greeting accompanied by the appropriate gesture) creates the emotion.

"To Be" and Yourself. There are two sides to the idea of "to be" energy: (1) the "to be" that you manufacture and (2) the "to be" that is the energy of the piece you are performing. These two energies often get confused when you perform.

Creating the energy of performing before you perform (i.e., artificially creating the "to be") becomes the problem. You feel you have to manufacture the energy of performance to do a good job. Your focus is, "What do I have to do to make this performance successful?"

The "to be" energy you manufacture has nothing to do with the "to be" energy of the piece. The "to be" energy that you manufacture is a general performance energy. It is excess excitement. It brings the focus onto the energy itself, instead of onto what you're doing. It is almost as if you manufacture it to protect yourself.

Instead of being open to the tone and/or emotional content of the piece, you create a generalized excitement or opening energy. This energy is nothing more than excess effort or tension. The tension makes you feel like the performance is going to be good. Without this tension, you feel naked.

But that nakedness is what dynamic performance is all about.

The way out of this paradox is bravery. You have to be brave enough to allow the performance to happen and then to trust that it will. To allow it to happen, you need to "take in," to listen, to use what is in front of you, to resonate with it.

Vulnerability. The stereotype of a sensitive person is that he or she is soft or weak. However, allowing yourself to be vulnerable is actually being fearless. If you are sensitive and open, if you include others versus excluding them, and if you include the possibility for change, you have courage, a fearless vulnerability.

Active and Passive Choices. In the theater, there are two kinds of approaches: active and passive. The active choice gives you more to do, so that you have more to experience. It makes your job easier. Passive choices give you less to do.

The passive choice to "make happiness" doesn't work because there is nothing for you to do, so you have nothing to experience. There is nothing doable.

In contrast, the active choice of "greeting the one I love" does work because you have something specific to do: the physical actions of opening your arms, embracing, and so on. The emotion is a by-product of the action of greeting and is supported by the physical activity of embracing.

The Two-Way Street. When you talk to someone, you are observing the person's face and reading their expressions as you talk. As you read the other person, you are making decisions about what you want to say next. Your thought process is rooted in the other person. Similarly, as you listen, you are reading the other person, and your face is communicating, whether you follow their point or not. It's a two-way street.

Many actors are watching themselves as they perform, instead of taking in the person or persons with whom they are trying to communicate. Simply put, the lesson here is that instead of watching yourself, you look at the person you are talking to, the person who is talking.

Who You Are vs. You as Performer

There is a difference between who you are and who you are when you perform.

Who Are You? When I first meet participants at a workshop, I often ask who they are and what they do. They will usually say, "My name is so-and-so, and I'm a conductor/musician/actor." Then I ask them to ask me who I am. And I'll tell them my name.

Then I ask them to ask me what I do, and I tell them, "I'm a husband, a father, a fly fisherman, a soccer coach, a house-maintenance man, and a part-time cook. Oh! And I also teach."

If my whole being is wrapped up in being one thing (e.g., a performer, a teacher, or a cellist), the stakes are too high. If the stakes are that high, no wonder it's so difficult to change.

Who Are You when You Perform? Who you are when you perform is a different matter from who you are. In chapter 1, I noted that when you perform, you are a vessel or conduit to the universal truth of humankind. You relate to every man or woman who has ever lived and to the human condition of our world. This is what allows you to dare to go for it.

When you are performing, what you are doing is the most important thing in the world and, at the same time, the least important (the world will not skip a beat if I am gone). The moments that I can create deserve my full and fearless presence.

Artistic Expression

"I never *practice*; I only perform." I believe the idea at the heart of this statement is a commitment to play with full artistic expression. The full intention of performing requires a certain specificity and energy. Merely "practicing" can mean a more general and less committed, less energetic approach.

Your commitment while practicing and performing is to be fearless in the face of judgment. While performing, you do not submit to the desire to do a good job or protect yourself from the possibility of failure. You proceed with fearless vulnerability.

Let me tell you a couple of stories about activities I use with my acting students to clarify the concept of intention and performance energy.

Commitment to Intention. The first simple activity I use in my classes is to have a student stand center stage, facing the audience. (If possible, I like to do this in a very large theater.) There is a chair ten feet to the student's right, at stage right.

I ask the student to move the chair about the same distance (ten feet) to stage left. This means the student is moving the chair roughly twenty feet from its original position. The student will happily comply.

I then ask the student to move the chair back to its stage right position. The student moves the chair. I ask the student to move the chair left again, then right again, and so on.

What happens is that, very quickly, the space between stage right and stage left starts to become smaller and smaller. If I kept at it long enough (which I don't), I'm sure the chair eventually would move only a couple of feet. We get tired.

But it seems to me that our job is to move the chair the full twenty feet each time. Now we are talking about the expenditure of energy. Am I willing to make that commitment to my intention every time?

Intention in the Moment. Another example of performance energy is a simple assignment I give to my beginning students. This time, we are in my studio, and everyone is in a corner of the room. I ask the students to walk, one at a time, to the center of the room, stop there and say their names, and then proceed diagonally to the opposite corner.

What do you think happens? The first student will do the exercise as described, then the second student does the same. As the students complete the exercise, a line starts to form along the wall. When the line gets to be about five or six people long, the exercise mysteriously changes.

The rest of students walk to the center, stop, and say their names. But now, instead of walking to the opposite corner after saying their names, the students walk immediately to the end of the line.

As the line grows, the angle of each student's departure from the center becomes more acute. Finally, the last few students say their names and then actually turn ninety degrees to exit.

Is this new direction chosen because the students' objective is to get the exercise over? Is it laziness? Or do the students not even know they are doing it?

Their intention changes. They get ahead of the moment. Instead of "walking to the corner," their intention becomes "getting to the end of the line."

Quite often when actors audition, their objective is just to get to the end of the piece. They just want to get through it. As a result, the audition piece becomes general, and everything between the beginning and the end comes out the same.

Interestingly enough, though the piece is performed quicker than if the actor had taken time to experience his or her intention for each line, it seems to go on forever to the observer.

When the performer actually works his or her way through the piece moment by moment, even though it may take a little longer to perform, we experience that piece as taking less time, because it is more specific and consequently more compelling to listen to and to watch.

Focus on Intention. As I discussed in chapter 1, it takes more work to exclude than to include. To put the focus on yourself, you have to exclude everything else. I have observed that this exclusion makes the body static. With an open focus, you include, and the process is dynamic.

You want to take the focus off of how you are doing and put your focus onto your intention, on what is doable. What is doable is experiencing the action of your intention in the moment as you do it.

In other words, when you focus on what is doable (the active choice), you will be in the moment. Simply put, do what you are doing.

Judging in Relation to Being in the Moment

Experience is in the moment. Being "right" (a judgment) happens before or after the moment.

Judgment is outside the moment, because when you are judging, that is all you are doing—judging.

Judging has nothing to do with performing and actually blocks your ability to experience what you are doing and remain in the moment. Judging is a single focus on you. It excludes everything else.

Judgment and Observation. Judging yourself is not helpful, because your focus is on judging yourself instead of performing. A generalized judgment is not useful information.

Making an observation of what you are actually doing is helpful, because there is no right or wrong attached to your specific observation. You take the information given to you and analyze it for yourself.

Judgment excludes, while observations include.

Judging vs. Experiencing. After a musical performance, we sometimes hear a performer ask, "How did I do?" The question I'd like to hear is, "How was the music?"

When I was studying classical acting, the dictum was, "Subordinate your self to the text. You aren't important; it's what you are doing that's important." Get the focus off of yourself and put it on what you're doing.

When learning to change the way you move or perform a role or conduct a piece of music, it's natural for you to wonder, "How am I doing?" which leads to asking, "How do I look?"

But this focus on judging yourself excludes the really pertinent questions: "What is going on? What is happening? What am I doing?"

You become more concerned with the visual results—how you are perceived—than with experiencing what you are doing (enacting a character's actions, sensing the music you are conducting, etc.).

I believe that watching yourself and wondering, "What does it look like?" leads you down the path to judgment. This question is not really so far away from "How am I doing?" or "Am I right?" These questions take you out of the moment.

Watching and/or judging yourself blocks movement, because while you are judging yourself, the surface of your body usually becomes still (i.e., you are holding). You exclude the outside world, perhaps to get a better look at yourself.

Instead of taking in what is going on around you (soft focus) and being involved in what you are supposed to be experiencing (playing/conducting/performing), you are judging yourself.

The job of the performer is to experience the act of playing/conducting/performing, not to judge or watch that performance.

Learning Skills. One way we learn skills is from watching our teachers. So it is not so great a jump from watching the teacher and seeing how they look to asking, "How do I look?"

Perhaps a more useful approach would be to ask, "How do they do that? How do I do that?" In the theater, we ask, "What am I doing?" When you are concentrating on how the performance looks, there is no experiencing a gesture or activity.

Being Right. In rehearsal, I find that the actors are more sometimes concerned with wanting to be "right" than with considering what they are "doing." Being right is (or seems) easier than learning how to improve, because it can be accomplished with tension, which, again, makes us feel as if we are doing a good job. Saying you want to be right can mean you want to make what you are doing *look* right and that all you are concerned with satisfying is your visual sense.

In contrast, improving what you are doing requires you to get inside the activity. You have to make a tactile, experiential connection.

Being right is a single focus: the single focus is on your self. There is no "taking in." Being right excludes everything but the focus on how you can be right.

Quick Fix. Out of fear, performers choose to block instead of experiencing what they are doing. Too often, performers try to control what is going on and to be "right" by tightening joints. The thinking of a performer who does this is simple: "I can completely close off and be 'good' by using a lot of effort; it will look 'right' if it doesn't move; it will be 'fixed.'"

However, this quick fix is not a permanent solution to your movement and performing problems. This approach is another way of excluding.

Answer to the Quick Fix. The answer to the quick fix is the opposite of excluding. The solution is to "take in" (include). In order to "take in" while you perform, you have to *trust yourself.* Trust that what you are doing is good enough. When you do include/"take in" while you perform, you no longer have time to watch/judge yourself. You can't take in and close off at the same time. It has to be one or the other.

The leap to make is giving up wanting to be right. This will set you free of judgment. You just don't have time for judging. You are busy doing what you are doing.

Sorting It Out. If you are spending time and exerting effort in judging, how can you sort out intention, availability, and following the weight shift with economy of effort, balance, and flow.

When you are judging, there is no pathway to collect feedback, because you are blocking experience. You're watching yourself.

What you are doing is then replaced with asking, "How am I doing?" As we've already pointed out, asking this question blocks experience. It is the slippery slope to wanting to be right.

The questions to ask are

"What is happening?"
"What is obvious?"
"What is going on?"
"What am I taking in?"
"What do I notice?"

When you ask, "How does this feel?" you go right back to focusing on yourself again. You wonder, "Does it feel correct?" Of course, a changed movement is not going to feel "correct" initially, because it is not yet familiar or habitual. It is not what you normally do. The new way is not habitual.

When change becomes habitual, then you've really got something.

Performance Problems

Over the years, I have found that certain performance problems are common to many actors/performers.

Facial Focus. Your face is a by-product of what you are experiencing. It is not where your performance starts and certainly not the place where you initiate emotions. Your emotions are reflected in your face. Be careful that your face doesn't become a single focus. The focus is on your entire being.

General Gestures. When I work with conductors, I often see general gestures. The problem with general conducting gestures is that they can usually work for any piece and anywhere in that piece. They are not specific to the moment. Because they are general, they don't allow you to experience the specific moment you are in. The same is true for general gestures by actors, singers, and others.

Copying Great Performers. I have noticed that conductors often copy great conductors' gestures. Other performers also copy their role models, so the following information applies to all performers. Conductors just serve as a particularly good example of what happens when you copy others' gestures.

The origin of the copied gesture came from the *original conductor* experiencing the moment. However, when you copy the gesture, you are "doing the movement" (focusing on how the gesture looked to you and how you are trying to make it look), and that intention blocks *you* from experiencing the moment.

You need to allow your own gestures to come from experiencing the moment, even though that means they most likely will be different from the great conductor you so admire. How often have we heard this advice: "You need to make it your own."

The purpose of each gesture is to clarify your intention and experience. You allow your gestures to come from your intention.

Overcoming Nervousness. If you are nervous or afraid, that is what you are doing—being nervous or afraid.

When you perform, it is not about you. It is about what you are doing, what you are experiencing. Put your focus on what you are doing. Experience what you are doing. If you include what is going on around you, you won't have time or energy to be nervous or afraid.

Compensations for Stillness. When you remove the compensations for imbalance and stillness, you have movement. To remove the compensations, you must become aware of them. You need to open yourself to the possibility for change. Then you can have a choice between the old way and the new way.

Change

Over the years, I have taught and been part of many different types of workshops. I have observed participants coming to workshops with the intention, I assume, to improve their skills. They want to become a better conductor, flute player, violinist, singer, equestrian, actor, athlete, and so on—to better whatever skill a workshop is designed to improve.

But I've noticed that very few workshop participants will initially come with the desire to change their process (i.e., what they are doing and how they are doing it). Everyone wants to get better, but no one wants to change how or what they are doing. It seems to me that what the participants are really after is validation for what they are already doing. They want to be told that what they are doing is good and that they are doing it well.

Think about it. If you really want to improve, something has to change; and that change must be made by you.

I tell my first-year students at the university, "If in four years you are acting the same way that you are acting now, then in four years you will be a high school actor." This is another way of saying, "If at the end of the workshop you are doing the same things you did before you took the workshop, what have you accomplished?"

Why is change so difficult for us? Allowing ourselves to change is the real struggle. At times, this struggle is heartbreaking to watch, because people keep holding themselves back, afraid to leave what is comfortable and familiar. What makes the struggle so heartbreaking is that, in the final analysis, it comes down to one question: what are you risking? You risk nothing, really. But at the time, in the heat of the moment when you are facing the prospect of actually changing, it seems as if you are risking everything.

I remind you of what Aldous Huxley said in *The Art of Seeing:* "Two things get in our way: fear of failure and wanting to do a good job." Really, they are both just two sides of the same coin.

The Process of Change. The longer you stay with the old way, the longer the process of change will take. You've got to incorporate change into your daily life. Otherwise, you are just kidding yourself.

Of course, you have to know how to change. You can't do it by being "right," and you can't do it by judging yourself. You change by accepting the new process: you substitute observation for judgment; you substitute movement for holding; you try to gain awareness of the obvious. Judgment blocks the obvious.

The Story of the Grocery Store. Let's say you want to find a grocery store, so you ask directions. You're told, "Go down to the end of the street, turn, and you'll find it." So you go down to the end of the street and turn left, and you find the post office. The next day, you go down to the corner, turn left, and find the post office and a gas station. The third day, you go down to the corner, turn left, and find the post office, the gas station, and a Chinese restaurant.

Now it's getting familiar. You know what to expect, and you feel comfortable. But you haven't found the grocery store. The only way to find the grocery store is to turn right. When you turn right, it isn't familiar or comfortable, but that's where you'll find the grocery store. The question then becomes, how long are you going to keep turning left?

Why Change Is So Frustrating. The reason change becomes so frustrating is that to effect a real change, you have to modify your process. That feels unfamiliar and uncomfortable. The activity that you are changing (general movement, conducting, playing an instrument, acting, etc.) isn't as simple anymore. You can't just do it the same old way.

Ultimately, once the change is incorporated into your movement patterns, it will be easier. But when you are threatened with change, all you see is the fact that you have to move/perform in a different way. Initially, you don't see the expected results.

Change implies that what you have been doing must not have been "right," which plays into your fear of failure. You were doing it (conducting, acting, playing) "wrong." It's harder to try a new way while you are defending your old way.

Remember that if your goal is to be "right," you are lost. The goal is to experience what you are doing while you are doing it.

Making Change Easier. We've all had moments when it "just happened."

When it's not happening, it is because your body isn't fully available. It isn't moving, you work against yourself, there is no flow, and it becomes difficult. You try harder, and the more you try, the less of your body moves.

When you get out of your own way, whatever you're doing (playing the violin, conducting an orchestra, performing on stage) becomes easier. This is when it "just happens."

The arrow shoots itself.
—ZEN SAYING

Observations on Performing

Many of the concepts discussed in this book can be summed up by the following observations on performing.

It seems that everyone wants to improve his or her performance by limiting movement. But improvement results from allowing movement.

Explore the compensations for imbalance. Erase these compensations.

How do you work on your technique? Focus on *what* you are doing, not *how* you are doing.

Experience the specific instead of trying to perform the general (i.e., you can't perform the whole play on every line).

You cannot increase your sensitivity unless you reduce your effort.

Sensitivity is not weakness; it is fearlessness.

Learning is not about how you are doing; it is about experiencing what you are doing.

Trying harder is a block.

Trying to be "right" wastes time and energy and isn't a worthwhile objective anyway.

For the most part, what stands in your way is a bunch of stuff that you don't have to do in the first place.

We are after uncluttered intention.

You act actions and ideas, not words.

Beginning artists are sequential; advanced artists are simultaneous.

What you do is what you do.

Eyes take in; they do not beam or direct focus.

Think of yourself in three dimensions versus two dimensions.

Fear of failure blocks success.

Wanting to do a good job is not an achievable objective. You cannot *do* (i.e., perform) a "good job."

A good job is the by-product of experiencing the moment.

You experience the specificity of your intention.

It's all a balancing act.

Experience what you are doing.

Posture is the body in motion.

Everything is moving.

Everything Is Moving

The vehicle to achieve all of the above is simply to allow your body to be alive as you perform. Allow a movable line of balance and counterbalance, so that you might perform with an economy of force and flow.

The more dramatically powerful a scene is, the greater the call on your inner forces, the freer your body must be.

— CONSTANTIN STANISLAVSKI, IN STANISLAVSKI
AND PAVEL RUMYANTSEV, *Stanislavski on Opera*

Appendix: Other Ideas That Influence Movement

When the mind's free, the body's delicate.
— WILLIAM SHAKESPEARE, *King Lear*

There are countless ideas and assumptions, both conscious and unconscious, that influence how we move and consequently affect our capacity for expression. Following are a few for your consideration.

Aesthetics

One of the primary ideas that affect how we move is a desire to have an attractive, aesthetic appearance. To achieve this aesthetic appearance, you first consider how you think you should look. Then you start holding yourself in a way that you think will allow you to get that look.

Holding our bodies in a particular posture in order to look the way we think we're supposed to look is a major source of body tension. We might even look a little better. But we do not *move* better.

Many people are holding their stomachs in to look thinner. The truth is that when you hold yourself, you are engaging muscles, and as the muscles compress, they look bulkier.

When you try to make yourself look a certain way by holding, you are actually working against yourself and making it harder to achieve your desired effect.

Vitality without Tension

It's the paradox of athletics. Tension is slow, tension is inefficient.
— COACH RICK DEMONT

I believe that people can subconsciously choose to create tension for the benefit of others. It is a way to show others that you are ready to go, that you are on your toes, that you are paying attention. I have seen coaches and trainers demand this state of tension from their students/players. Unfortunately, though this helps the coach feel that his team is geared up to win, it does not help the player's or the team's performance.

What we're looking for is vitality without tension. Any type of tension will cause you to lose suspension. When you lose suspension, every movement you make requires more effort and becomes less efficient. With tension, there is constriction, which causes more wear and tear on the joint itself.

When you are tense, you lose fluidity of movement and expression, because you have shortened your muscles. Basic physiology dictates that the longer the muscle is, the stronger it is, and the shorter the muscle is, the weaker it is.

If the muscle isn't tense, it remains longer and therefore has more capacity to contract. Having more of your muscle available to contract means that more of your body is available for creative expression.

Your Objective Is to Play. So what happens when your favorite team falls behind? The goal shifts from playing to catching up or winning. Players then tense to achieve the goal of winning, but rarely do they catch up and win. I believe this is because they are after the wrong objective.

In order to win, you must play well. You cannot play well with tension and shortened muscles. The objective is always to play well. Winning is a by-product. This is what people mean when they say that it's not whether you win or lose, it's how you play the game.

Put succinctly, if you shorten, you lose.

The Confessional Moment

When teaching physical expression, I'll often hear what I call "the confessional moment." It is a time when a student confesses to me a belief that a parent or instructor has told him or her—maybe years ago. After a few weeks or months of our working together, the student questions that belief. Up until the confessional moment, that belief has affected how the person moves.

A good friend and former student of mine could not get movement in her pelvis. As a horsewoman, she needed motion in her pelvis if she wanted to progress with her sport. After a few months, she finally said to me, "But my riding instructor told me to tuck my pelvis."

It is important to point out that this was *her* interpretation of what her riding instructor actually said. However, as long as she held on to her conception of that idea, she would continue to tuck and hold her pelvis and not allow movement.

Soon after our conversation, she started getting movement through her hips and legs, and eventually she relaxed and allowed her pelvis to move while riding. Until that confessional moment when she gave up her belief that she had to tuck her pelvis and hold it in place, she really had no chance of change.

The greater the singer's concentration on the complete sound image, the more relaxed his body seems to become.

—SERGIUS KAGEN, *On Studying Singing*

Automatic Response: Fight or Flight

The almost reflexive tightening that we do before beginning any movement or activity is a habitual response. We tighten up and then begin the movement.

Some people would argue that this automatic tightening is connected to the fight-or-flight response (the automatic pattern of protection that we go into when we are threatened). Our body grips and curls inward to protect our head and vital organs. It's an immediate response in the face of emergency. It is not an efficient way to move.

Think of your body as having circuit breakers. With the fight-or-flight response, you hit the grand master, and everything is engaged. All muscles are tensed. It's not a matter of life or death to get out of a chair, turn a page, or chop a carrot. So there's no need to enter a fight-or-flight mode to accomplish everyday tasks.

Every time you move, you do not want to automatically tighten muscles that are not needed. Firing unnecessary muscles impedes your movement and hampers your ability to be expressive. We want to engage only the muscles that facilitate our intention and no more.

Senses Take In

Notice that when we really want to concentrate, we try to hold the world still. We tense and hold our bodies to better maintain focus, but what we forget is that all our senses receive. They take in information. Our senses do not go out and grab.

We've noted that vision is not a laser beam. Even though we think we are looking out at the world, we are actually absorbing light. Ears take in as well. We allow the music in.

For example, I often see musicians straining, bent forward and "focused" on their sheet music. Then I remind them that their eyes take in, and they realize what they have been doing to themselves in order to focus on the music. Suddenly, their bodies relax. Immediately the music sounds better. A beneficial by-product is that the musician will have less of the pain that is caused by tension and excess effort. "Taking in" allows the process of performing to be easier.

All our senses take in by their very nature. When we perform, we resonate outward from within.

Thinking without Tension. When people really want to concentrate, they often compress their bodies. Some will habitually tense in order to listen or think. But once you tense, it's all over; that is, when the body tenses, the mind tenses, restricting the mental activity of listening or thinking. If you are more relaxed while in a discussion with someone, you can actually hear what he or she has to say.

If there is movement in the body, there can be movement in the mind.

Speaking Is Vibrating. Take a moment and think about how you produce sound. As you stand there, all you really need to do is allow your vocal cords to vibrate as air passes over them. Yet speakers all across the country (either to do a good job, to be heard, or to get their excitement across to their audience) constrict their bodies before they begin to speak.

To demonstrate this phenomenon, I sometimes take my students into one of our larger theaters and ask who can project his or her voice from the stage all the way to the back of the house. The volunteer typically prepares, takes a huge breath, tenses, and goes for it.

Now wait a minute. Think about this. If sound is created by vibrating, and if your whole body is designed to vibrate while you speak, why tense, constrict everything, and limit your capacity to vibrate?

As I tell my students, the tension you create is for yourself, not for your audience. It makes you feel as if you're really "doing it" (projecting, working, acting). But the tension you create to make yourself feel like you will succeed actually stands between you and your audience.

Language

Language can affect how we move, just as the words we use to describe movement reflect our beliefs and thoughts about movement.

The following common phrases reveal how connected to movement our language is:

"He's in a slump."
"Wow, is she uptight."
"Get ahold of yourself."
"Keep your chin up."
"Stay on your toes."

It is interesting that almost all of these phrases involve stopping movement. All of these ideas affect how we move, even if they do so at a subtle level.

Wouldn't it be nice if, instead of hearing language that hinders our movement and disempowers us, we heard, "Balance. Economize your effort. Let everything work together."

Words Reveal the Truth. When I work with my students, instead of focusing only on the idea that they are trying to communicate, I listen to the specific word choices they make.

A classic example illustrates how the words that are used reveal what a person is truly saying. A student said to me, "Now I know it's not a position, but where do I put my pelvis?" The key word in the sentence is *put*. What the student really said was, "I know I'm not supposed to believe in positioning or holding, but what is the position? How can I make this right?"

I have noticed that my students' use of language reflects how they're progressing. When they stop talking about putting body parts in the right place and start using words like *allow* (as in "allow movement," "allow weight to shift naturally"), it's clear to me that they are internalizing the lesson. When their language changes, so do their bodies.

The Trap of Fixing

Another phenomenon I've observed is what I call "directional release." It involves the idea of determining where you think the body parts should go as you release tension. You attempt to achieve that "perfect" look by releasing tension and then consciously helping the body parts move in the "right" direction.

Your thought process goes like this: "I'm going to relax this holding spot and put this body part right there so my posture looks better." A few examples of directional release follow.

Example 1. I once worked with a male violinist who was having shoulder problems. When I looked at him, it wasn't difficult to see that, thanks to tension, his left shoulder was up around his ears. I helped him relax his shoulder.

At the next appointment, guess what I noticed? His shoulder was pushed down—the direction of release that he became aware of when he learned to relax. The direction wasn't wrong, but the act of pushing negated any good achieved by releasing the tension in his shoulders.

Here's what happened: When the violinist relaxed his shoulder to release the tension, he noticed that it was now lower than it had been when he was tense. This is an accurate observation. But his mistake was thinking he needed to make an effort to lower his shoulder.

That "fixing" effort required more tension, as the violinist focused on pushing the shoulder into the "right" position. The efficient strategy would have been simply to have allowed the shoulder to be where it wanted to be when the tension was erased. There was no need to fix.

The point of this example is that as the violinist relaxed his shoulder, there was more movement potential. When he consciously "corrected" the position of his shoulder lower, he limited his movement, so he wasn't really any better off. Instead of positioning, all he had to do was trust his body.

Example 2. A friend came to me with a stiff neck, and I helped him notice what wasn't moving. As the muscles relaxed, my friend tried to push his head up to where he thought it was supposed to go. This is another example of trying to put a body part where you think it should go after experiencing the relaxation of tension: you substitute one limitation for another (with the best of intentions, of course).

The thing to remember is that even though movement follows when tension is released, you will restrict movement if you try to place your body in the position that results from that release.

Also, you can't predict in what direction a particular body part is supposed to go, because when you release tension, you are releasing muscles into motion in relation to the rest of the body.

If a body part moves, the movement is in relation to what's happening with the rest of your body, and the part does not necessarily go where you think it ought to end up. The following awareness study uses an extreme example to illustrate my point.

AWARENESS STUDY: Directional Release

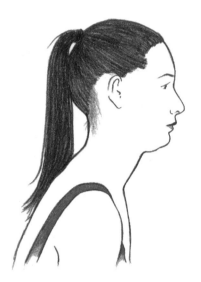

1. Slump way down through your chest, head, and neck.
2. Now, without any movement in your torso, try to put only your head where it is "supposed" to go for "perfect" posture.
3. Notice the tension in your neck that results from trying to position the head.

Even though you are trying to put your head where you know it is supposed to go, it doesn't work, because your upper torso is still slumping. Your head can't get to where it needs to be in order to be supported by the torso.

Unless you also allow movement to integrate with the whole body (all the parts that were compensating as a result of your head being held several inches forward), your attempt to achieve perfect posture isn't going to be very effective, is it?

One last example. If a person is standing with his or her pelvis forward of balance and releases only the tension in the lower back, he or she will move forward, not back toward "perfect" posture. You can see this movement demonstrated in this illustration.

New Information in an Old Context

As you gain new awareness and the potential for new movement options, the challenge becomes how to fit this new awareness into your old context of moving habitually, a context made up of how the movement feels to you as well as your concepts and ideas about movement. You can't accomplish this. Attempting to do so is wasted energy. The more time you spend trying to fit this new information into your old thought streams, the longer the river will become.

Take each new experience for what it is—not what you think it should be, how you think it should work, or what you think the result should be.

Conclusion

It's important to consider what the thoughts that influence our movement patterns are actually doing to our bodies.

All the ideas about wanting to look good and fixing our posture were meant to be helpful. There is even a grain of truth behind them.

But these ideas are based on achieving an end product, and they skip the process needed to get there. They are after a static picture versus a dynamic performance.

As performers, our goal is to move with balance and an economy of force while allowing flow to enhance our capacity for expression.

Bibliography

Albinus, Bernhard Siegfried. *Tabulae sceleti et musculorum corporis humani*. London: Printed by H. Woodfall for J. and P. Knapton, 1749.

Anderson, Bob. *Stretching*. Illustrated by Jean Anderson. Bolinas, California: Shelter Publications, 1980.

Barker, Sarah. *The Alexander Technique: Learning to Use Your Body for Total Energy*. New York: Bantam Books, 1978. Reprint, 1991.

Barlow, Wilfred. *The Alexander Principle*. London: Victor Gollancz, 1973.

Barrault, Jean-Louis. *Memories for Tomorrow: The Memoirs of Jean-Louis Barrault*. New York: E. P. Dutton and Company, 1974.

Bartenieff, Irmgard. *Body Movement: Coping with the Environment*. New York: Gordon and Breach Science Publishers, 1980.

Becker, Robert O., and Gary Selden. *The Body Electric: Electromagnetism and the Foundation of Life*. Illustrated by David Bichell. New York: William Morrow and Company, 1985.

Berry, Cicely. *Voice and the Actor*. New York: Macmillan Publishing Company, 1973.

Boleslavsky, Richard. *Acting: The First Six Lessons*. New York: Theatre Arts Books, 1933. Reprint, 1982.

Bond, Mary. *Rolfing Movement Integration: A Self-Help Approach to Balancing the Body*. Rochester, Vermont: Healing Arts Press, 1993.

Bridgman, George B. *Constructive Anatomy*. 1920. Reprint, New York: Dover Publications, 1973.

Brook, Peter. *The Empty Space*. London: MacGibbon and Kee, 1968.

Brook, Peter. "The Physical Life of the Actor." Interview with Kenneth Rae, *Drama* 3, no. 153 (1984): 16.

Calais-Germain, Blandine. *Anatomy of Movement*. Translated by Nicole Commarmond. Seattle: Eastland Press, 1993.

Christensen, Alice. *The American Yoga Association Beginner's Manual*. New York: Simon and Schuster, Fireside, 1987.

Conable, Barbara, and Ben Conable. *What Every Musician Needs to Know about the Body*. Portland, Oregon: Andover Press, 1998. Revised edition, 2000.

Conable, Barbara, and William Conable. *How to Learn the Alexander Technique: A Manual for Students*. Columbus, Ohio: Andover Road Press, 1992.

Couch, Jean. *The Runner's Yoga Book: A Balanced Approach to Fitness*. Berkeley, California: Rodmell Press, 1990.

Dell, Cecily. *A Primer for Movement Description*. New York: Dance Notation Bureau Press, 1977.

Dintiman, George, Bob Ward, and Tom Tellez. *Sports Speed*. With a foreword by Leroy Burrell. Champaign, Illinois: Human Kinetics, 1998.

Dowd, Irene. *Taking Root to Fly: Articles on Functional Anatomy.* Northampton, Massachusetts: Contact Editions, 1981. Reprint, 1990.

Dychtwald, Ken. *Bodymind.* With a foreword by Marilyn Ferguson. Los Angeles: Jeremy P. Tarcher, 1977. Reprint, 1986.

Einstein, Albert. *Ideas and Opinions.* Based on *Mein Weltbild*, edited by Carl Seelig, and other sources. New translations and revisions by Sonja Bargmann. New York: Wings Books, 1988.

Enters, Angna. *On Mime.* Middletown, Connecticut: Wesleyan University Press, 1965.

Fahey, Brian W. *The Power of Balance: A Rolfing View of Health.* Portland, Oregon: Metamorphous Press, 1989.

Feldenkrais, Moshé. *Awareness through Movement.* New York: Harper and Row, 1972. Reprint, 1977.

Feldenkrais, Moshé. *Body and Mature Behaviour.* Madison, Connecticut: International Universities Press, 1988.

Feldenkrais, Moshé. *The Elusive Obvious.* Cupertino, California: Meta Publications, 1981.

Feldenkrais, Moshé. *The Master Moves.* Cupertino, California: Meta Publications, 1984.

Feldenkrais, Moshé. *The Potent Self: A Guide to Spontaneity.* Edited by Michaeleen Kimmey. San Francisco: Harper and Row, 1985.

Felner, Mira. *Apostles of Silence.* Rutherford, New Jersey: Fairleigh Dickinson University Press, 1985.

Fo, Dario. *The Tricks of the Trade.* Translated by Joe Farrell. Edited and with notes by Stuart Hood. New York: Routledge, 1991.

Friedman, Philip, and Gail Eisen. *The Pilates Method of Physical and Mental Conditioning.* Garden City, New York: Doubleday and Company, 1980.

Gelb, Michael. *Body Learning: An Introduction to the Alexander Technique.* With a preface by Laura Huxley. New York: Henry Holt and Company, 1981. Reprint, 1987.

Gray, Henry. *Anatomy: Descriptive and Surgical.* Illustrated by H. V. Carter. 1858. Reprint, London: Grange Books, 2001.

Hale, Robert Beverly. *Drawing Lessons from the Great Masters.* New York: Watson-Guptill Publications, 1964. Reprint, 1989.

Hanna, Thomas. Somatics: *Reawakening the Mind's Control of Movement, Flexibility, and Health.* Reading, Massachusetts: Addison-Wesley Publishing Company, 1988. Reprint, 1990.

Heller, Joseph, and William A. Henkin. *Bodywise: Regaining Your Natural Flexibility and Vitality for Maximum Well-Being.* Los Angeles: Jeremy P. Tarcher, 1986.

Herrigel, Eugen. *Zen in the Art of Archery.* Translated by R. F. C. Hull. With an introduction by D. T. Suzuki. New York: Random House, Vintage Books, 1971.

Huxley, Aldous. *The Art of Seeing.* 1942. Reprint, with a foreword by Laura Huxley, Berkeley, California: Creative Arts Book Company, 1982.

Johnstone, Keith. *Impro: Improvisation and the Theatre.* With an introduction by Irving Wardle. New York: Theatre Arts Books, 1981.

Jones, Frank Pierce. *A Study of the Alexander Technique: Body Awareness in Action.* New York: Schocken Books, 1976.

Jou, Tsung Hwa. *The Tao of Tai-Chi Chuan: Way to Rejuvenation.* Edited by Shoshana Shapiro. Warwick, New York: Tai Chi Foundation, 1988.

Juhan, Deane. *Job's Body: A Handbook for Bodywork.* Barrytown, New York: Station Hill Press, 1987.

Kagen, Sergius. *On Studying Singing.* New York: Dover Publications, 1960.

Kapandji, I. A. *The Physiology of the Joints.* Volumes 1–3. Translated by L. H. Honore. New York: Churchill Livingstone, 1982.

Laban, Rudolf. *The Mastery of Movement.* Revised by Lisa Ullmann. Boston: Plays, 1971.

Maisel, Edward. *The Alexander Technique: The Essential Writings of F. Matthias Alexander.* New York: Carol Communications, 1967. Reprint, 1989.

Mechner, Vicki. *Healing Journeys: The Power of Rubenfeld Synergy.* Chappaqua, New York: OmniQuest Press, 1998.

Musashi, Miyamoto. *A Book of Five Rings.* Translated by Victor Harris. Woodstock, New York: Overlook Press, 1974.

Myers, Thomas. *The Anatomical Illustrations of John Hull Grundy.* Chibolton, Hampshire, United Kingdom: Noble Books, 1983.

Olivier, Lawrence. *On Acting.* New York: Simon and Schuster, 1986.

Pecknold, Adrian. *Mime: The Step Beyond Words.* Revised edition, with a preface by Michael Langham. Toronto: NC Press, 1989.

Rodenburg, Patsy. *The Actor Speaks.* London: Methuen Drama, 1997.

Rolf, Ida P. *Rolfing and Physical Reality.* Edited and with an introduction by Rosemary Feitis. Rochester, Vermont: Healing Arts Press, 1978, 1990.

Rolf, Ida P. *Rolfing: Reestablishing the Natural Alignment and Structural Integration of the Human Body for Vitality and Well-Being.* Rochester, Vermont: Healing Arts Press, 1989.

Rubins, David K. *The Human Figure: An Anatomy for Artists.* New York: Penguin Books, 1976.

Rywerant, Yochanan. *The Feldenkrais Method: Teaching by Handling.* New Canaan, Connecticut: Keats Publishing, 1983.

Schider, Fritz. *An Atlas of Anatomy for Artists.* Revised by M. Auerbach. Translated by Bernard Wolf. New York: Dover Publications, 1957.

Shawn, Ted. *Every Little Movement: A Book about Francois Delsarte.* Brooklyn, New York: Dance Horizons, 1963.

Solomon, Eldra Pearl, and P. William Davis. William. *Understanding Human Anatomy and Physiology.* New York: McGraw-Hill Book Company, 1978.

Spolin, Viola. *Improvisation for the Theater.* Evanston, Illinois: Northwestern University Press, 1963. Reprint, 1983, 1999.

Stanislavski, Constantin. *An Actor Prepares.* Translated by Elizabeth Reynolds Hapgood. New York: Theatre Arts Books, 1936. Reprint, 1976.

Stanislavski, Constantin. *Building a Character.* Translated by Elizabeth Reynolds Hapgood. New York: Theatre Arts Books, 1949. Reprint, 1976.

Stanislavski, Constantin. *My Life in Art.* Translated by J. J. Robbins. New York: Theatre Arts Books, 1948.

Stanislavski, Constantin, and Pavel Rumyantsev. *Stanislavski on Opera.* Translated and edited by Elizabeth Reynolds Hapgood. New York: Routledge, 1998.

Strauch, Ralph. "The Feldenkrais Method and Posture." http://www.posturepage.com/feldenkrais/index.html.

Sweigard, Lulu E. *Human Movement Potential: Its Ideokinetic Facilitation.* Lanham, Maryland: Harper and Row, 1974.

Swift, Sally. *Centered Riding.* North Pomfret, Vermont: David and Charles, 1985.

Todd, Mabel E. *The Thinking Body: A Study of the Balancing Forces of Dynamic Man.* Princeton, New Jersey: Princeton Book Company, 1937.

Trager, Milton. *Trager Mentastics: Movement as a Way to Agelessness.* Barrytown, New York: Station Hill Press, 1987.

Zollner, Frank. *Leonardo da Vinci: Sketches and Drawings.* Cologne: Taschen, 2004.

Index

Illustrative material is shown in italics.